Lawn Tennis
THE AUSTRALIAN WAY

Lawn Tennis
THE AUSTRALIAN WAY

Edited by Jack Pollard

Drake Publishers Inc   New York

LCCCN 72-6835

ISBN 0-87749-368-5

Published in 1973 by
Drake Publishers Inc
381 Park Avenue South
New York, N.Y. 10016

© Lansdowne Press, 1973

Printed in Hong Kong

Frontispiece   Rod Laver
Jacket   Evonne Goolagong

CONTENTS

1 THE CHALLENGE OF LAWN TENNIS

Wayne Reid

As a tennis player Wayne Vivian Reid was a rare crowd-pleaser, a giant (6 ft 1 in. 16 stone), black-haired Victorian with exceptional serving power who regularly upset fancied players at the big tournaments. At the 1962 South Australian championships in Adelaide, for instance, he defeated Rod Laver, now recognised as the world's greatest player. He slipped out of the tennis spotlight not long after that big win, however, to concentrate on business. By the time he was elected president of The Lawn Tennis Association of Australia in 1969 he was a director of several big companies and newspapers, rightly or wrongly, spoke of him as a self-made millionaire. Australian tennis fans, aware that Reid's opinions differed to those of Harry Hopman and 'Big Bill' Edwards hoped that Reid would give our tennis administration a new look. In the toughest job in Australian sport, and in the most difficult years Australian tennis has known, Reid has not disappointed. He has put forth a stream of aggressive ideas. It was Reid who advocated the appointment of a full-time Australian tournaments promotions officer, and he had his way when John Brown, 29, champion of Reid's club, South Yarra, was appointed to the job. Several times when big sponsorships were needed to save important tournaments, Reid's big business persuasiveness has pulled it off. In 1970, he was elected unopposed for a second term as president. Despite the demands of his family (he has two small children, Amanda and Nicholas) and of his company directorships, he has brought to the L.T.A.A. presidency a vigour and a clearsightedness that prevented a bad period in our tennis from becoming even worse. Tennis in Australia may have a long way to go before it gets out of its current difficulties but almost to a man Australian tennis players were glad Reid was at the helm in such hazardous years.

Tennis, in my view is the greatest sport of all—a game for everyone—regardless of age, race or religion. Around the world millions of people play the game. In Australia alone, more than 400,000 people play tennis regularly as members of clubs and thousands more play it socially. There are now ninety-three nations in the International Lawn Tennis Federation, and every year more than fifty nations take part in the Davis Cup competition.

Australian tennis today has the best men and women players in the world. Since 1939, Australia has won sixteen of the twenty-five Davis Cup competitions played. In a great run between 1950 and 1968 Australia overcame nine challenges from the U.S.A., two each from Italy and Spain and one each from Mexico and India. Of the nine Federation Cup matches played, Australia has won five. The world's major championships over recent years have been consistently won by Australians.

Australia is a comparatively small nation by population, yet its tennis players earn unparalleled publicity in the world's daily press. In the remote corners of the world, in the big continents of Europe, Asia, Africa, North America, every day you will read of the feats of Australian tennis players.

Open tennis has placed the Australians among the top money-earners in any sport. Rod Laver earned $200,000 in prize money in 1970 and is reported to have doubled this from off-court income. Mrs Margaret Court is reported to have grossed over $100,000 in prize money. The next three ranking men in the world, all Australians, would all earn well in excess of $100,000 per year. Thus the professional aspect of the game has been made legitimate and is now being exploited by young Australians.

The background to this wonderful Australian achievement spans six decades from Sir Norman Brookes' first Australian Wimbledon singles title in 1914 to Rod Laver's second Grand Slam in 1969 and Margaret Court's Grand Slam in 1970. Much credit for Australia's success must be given to that band of honorary workers, thousands in number, who have given unlimited time and energy to the organisation of tennis at all levels. Some organised the first junior tournament in which champions took part, others local club events and team championships right through to the Australian championships, Davis Cup Challenge Rounds and Federation Cup competitions. Foremost of these diligent workers were Sir Norman Brookes, President of the L.T.A.A. for 29 years, Harry Hopman, Davis Cup player for five years and captain for

Rod Laver, whose earnings from tennis exceeded $200,000 in 1970. His off-court earnings probably enabled him to double that sum. Laver was launched from amateur coaching schemes.

Big-money boys of top-class tennis jokingly celebrate their prosperity with cigars. *Left to right,* Pancho Segura, Pancho Gonzales, Lew Hoad (with the matches), Frank Sedgman, Ken Rosewall, Mervyn Rose (at rear), Jack Kramer and Ashley Cooper.

twenty years, and recognised as an outstanding trainer of young tennis players throughout Australia. The men have not been the only contributors. Mrs Florence Conway and Mrs Nell Hopman will long be remembered particularly for their part in Australia's successful agitation for the establishment of the Federation Cup series.

The Lawn Tennis Association of Australia comprises the six State Tennis Associations. Its headquarters are in Melbourne to which city it moved in 1926 when Sir Norman Brookes was elected as President, an office he held until 1955. Because of the great distances to be travelled, and the costs involved, the two L.T.A.A. Councillors nominated by each State are Melbourne residents. Each year there is an Annual Conference attended by Councillors, State Presidents, and another State representative, with the express purpose of formulating the basic policy of the L.T.A.A. Council for the following year.

The L.T.A.A. is a member of the International Lawn Tennis Federation which, as mentioned earlier, now has ninety-three members. On this body Australia, because of its standing in world tennis, has twelve votes along with Great Britain, France and the United States of America. The voting rights were set after taking into consideration the standard of achievement of each country, the number of tennis players and the number of times the country has won the Davis Cup. Each of the top four countries can appoint a delegate to the I.L.T.F. Committee of Management. The other eighty-nine countries nominate the other seven members, with a formula for every tennis zone in the world to be represented on the I.L.T.F. Committee of Management. The other major international body is the Davis Cup Nations, comprising the sixty nations eligible to enter for the Davis Cup, and of which Australia is naturally a member.

The L.T.A.A. has never owned its own tennis courts, but has provided the State Associations with considerable finance from the profits of Davis Cup Challenge Rounds so assisting every State in Australia in building a first-rate tennis stadium—a situation unique in the world. This means that it has been possible for Davis Cup Challenge Rounds, Australian Championships and the Federation Cup, to be staged throughout the country and not to be restricted to the one major city, a policy of the L.T.A.A. designed to ensure the promotion of tennis in every State of Australia.

Many of the State associations have a history similar to that of the L.T.A.A. and many great names have participated in their formation and establishment. In recent years, we have seen the development of magnificent new headquarters in Hobart, five minutes from the city centre in the Domain, and a great achievement for Tasmanian President, Viv Holloway, a former Victorian who went south in the 1950s. In 1970 we saw the opening of the new Canberra tennis centre which will enable the A.C.T. to participate in some of the major tennis played in Australia, starting with the first national veterans' championship in 1971.

Tennis at present is going through a period of great change. We have seen the expansion of the original Jack

Kramer professional troupe into two groups, and the subsequent merger of these into one organisation under the control of Texan millionaire Lamar Hunt. This 'World Championship Tennis' group, now contains more than thirty-two players, and its influence on the game presents a great problem for international tennis administrators, especially when the decisions of one man can affect the ability of Australians to watch and enjoy the play of the very stars they helped create.

In our democratic world, it is unrealistic for one person to control the world's leading tennis players and to have the sole decision over when, where and for whom these stars should play. This is one facet of Open Tennis that would not have occurred had Opens been introduced earlier. However, the Hunt organisation is part of the world tennis scene and must be accepted as such.

One of Australia's biggest problems at present is our dependence on success in the Davis Cup, firstly in conveying our position as the leading tennis nation and secondly in financing our tennis development. This has been brought about because the Davis Cup is limited to those players who are not under contract to the professional promoters. The main argument advanced by other countries against opening the Davis Cup to all players is that Lamar Hunt would at his whim, withdraw his players at any time, possibly disrupting the entire competition and preventing a nation from winning the Cup.

Unfortunately for Australia, the present Davis Cup regulations prevent Australia's top fifteen players, including the top four players in the world, from representing us in Cup matches. I am hopeful that in future negotiations this will be overcome and the event condensed, thus enabling every player to participate, as it is essential that this, the recognised international teams' championship, should remain the premier tennis event of the world.

Certainly this was the case in the Frank Sedgman era and through the careers of players such as Lew Hoad, Mervyn Rose, Neale Fraser, and Ashley Cooper, when we saw world record attendances at Davis Cup Challenge Rounds in Sydney and Melbourne. At Sydney in 1954 25,587 people—the greatest crowd ever to watch a tennis match anywhere in the world—saw each day's play. The takings in Sydney were US$334,464 and another US$216,000 had to be returned to the public because all seats were sold. The Davis Cup stood alone then at the pinnacle of the tennis world.

The future of Australian tennis, and its present strength, is in the many individual clubs scattered through the suburbs and country districts, and probably headed by one of the greatest clubs in the world—Royal South Yarra in Melbourne—situated amongst the stately homes of Toorak, and founded in the Pat O'Hara Wood–Sir Norman Brookes' era. New clubs continue to be established in many new housing developments, and it is particularly encouraging to note the great co-operation between the State Associations and local councils ensuring that the recreation areas contain adequate tennis

Wayne Reid was elected President of The Lawn Tennis Association of Australia in 1969.

facilities. This has also occurred in country areas where more and more major tennis centres are appearing—notable among these being the development in the Albury–Wodonga area. Country areas, of course, have produced many of the greats. Rod Laver from Gladstone, Queensland, and Margaret Court from Albury, New South Wales, are the prime examples.

Australia's success has resulted in many overseas players visiting this country, and together with the Australian players' and coaches' influence in overseas countries, this must result in an equalisation of standards throughout the world. Additionally, European and Asian countries, now becoming completely re-established after the war-time slump, will exert a greater influence on world tennis as their standard improves. This will be to the overall benefit of the game, but I believe Australian players will continue to dominate world tennis.

The success of Australian tennis stems from two sources. Firstly, from the wonderful organisation which guides the player from his beginnings at club level right to the time he becomes a Davis Cup player, and, secondly, from the players themselves. Australian players are not allowed to become 'prima donnas' as some Europeans have, and this has been highlighted by their ability to keep fighting when others 'throw in the towel'. Australians in tennis have always shown great fighting spirit and their characteristic down to earth appraisal of their own ability has ensured their ready acceptance by all tournaments.

Australian tennis players have done, and will keep doing, a magnificent job for our country. Problems facing our administrators need to be solved quickly so that the public can easily understand the pros and cons of player categories, open tournaments and the Davis Cup situation. It's a big challenge but tennis must adjust to the era of the millionaire player.

2 CATCH THEM YOUNG
Dinny Pails

Denis Robert Pails was born in Nottingham, England, on 4 March 1921. He was the first major player developed in Australia after World War II. In 1946, he lost the Australian singles final after a tense three-hour duel with John Bromwich. He was Australia's main hope for that year's Wimbledon, but was delayed by traffic on his way to a Centre Court quarter-final against the Frenchman, Yvon Petra. Pails' late arrival unsettled him, and Petra won 7–5, 7–5, 6–8, 6–4. Pails won the 1947 Australian title, beating American Tom Brown and old rival Bromwich (4–6, 6–4, 3–6, 7–5, 8–6) in the final. He beat Falkenburg at the 1947 Wimbledon and was the only player to take a set from Kramer. He played singles in Davis Cup matches for Australia in 1946 and 1947. When Kramer turned professional soon afterwards, Pails joined him. Today, Dinny Pails can reflect on a successful professional career in which he made his family financially secure for life. He has become a highly successful coach, largely because of his warm understanding of children, and, apart from several headline-winning pupils, each year he introduces hundreds of Australian boys and girls to the sport. Beside helping Lew Hoad and Ken Rosewall in their steps towards world titles, Pails has been official coach to the U.S. Davis Cup team in Australia eight times. One year he coached three nations' Cup teams.

Today more Australian parents than ever before like having their offspring coached in tennis. They want their children to have a chance to become first-class players and they believe a good coach can make the way easier.

Often in my work with children at the courts I hear a parent say, 'I want my child to have every chance at tennis by being properly coached—something my own parents could not afford. I don't want to see my boy or girl get into bad habits.'

The parents are right to want their children shown the fundamentals of the game by an expert, but they frequently become impatient and start asking why their children aren't champions after a few lessons. These parents fail to realize that, although their boy or girl enjoys tennis, many children are not interested in putting in the hundreds of hours of hard work that produce champions. They should remember that there is no harm in tennis on a leisurely level—not everyone can be a champion.

Given a child who is really keen to practise hard, you have a sound basis on which to work. But the champion has to have other qualities, too—natural ability, a deep love of the game, a pride of performance, a fighting heart, the ability to concentrate, the ability to relax, a capacity for physical development through exercises.

Here are some of the common difficulties children face when they are learning to play tennis:—

A junior tennis squad practising the fundamentals of the game.

- Impractical rackets—often rackets are too heavy or too thick in the handle.
- Failure to concentrate. Children should not make a joke of their tennis, chatter or rag about it.
- Overplay. Some children by over-keenness stay too long on the court and, as they tire, get slower and more ragged in their stroke-making.
- Not enough play. It is not sufficient for children to go half-heartedly through the motions coaches describe, and then leave the court.
- Failure to correct faults before progressing to other aspects of the game.
- Inability to make contact with the ball through a lack of ball-sense or lazy foot-work.

On wet days, children can benefit from practising each stroke in front of a mirror, thinking about each stroke as they make it and watching for defects that may cause errors.

I am repeatedly asked by parents at what age a child should start to learn tennis. This depends entirely on the physical make-up of the child.

The problem of racket-weight is the major hurdle we coaches face in dealing with parents. Parents often insist that their own racket—'a bit old but good enough for a child'—should be used, at least until their offspring shows some form or grows a bit. You can imagine the difficulty experienced by little tots with tiny wrists and hardly any strength in wielding an adult's racket that may weigh too much even for a husky character like, say, Lew Hoad!

Ken McGregor discusses equipment more fully in his chapter, but I want to support his advice that children of ten or twelve, or of small physique, should always use junior models with small grips.

Good coaches should study the requirements of each pupil individually. Some years ago I had two outstanding juniors among my pupils, Kay Dening and Tony Roche, but each posed a different problem for me when I first began coaching them.

Kay had been with me since she was nine, and I had the job of building up her game right from the start. She was physically very small, and this meant we had to work out a programme of exercises for her to help her in sustaining rallies. She was not quick enough to go in to the net to volley, so we had to build up her ground-game and make the shots she used when the ball came to her really effective.

The next step was to improve her volley, so that she had confidence to go to the net. All of this was done to a background of school examinations, which Kay and her family rightly considered she should not neglect because of her tennis.

Tony Roche's game was well developed when he came to me, and in contrast to Kay Dening, my main job with him was to polish the diamond of his natural talent, to supply the finishing touches to a well-produced stroke-repertoire. Tony was a big, strong boy—a natural tennis-player—and, to give him experience, I took him with me when I toured the country giving clinics to children. This way, Tony played on concrete one day, clay or grass the next, sometimes on rough surfaces, sometimes on

courts a little sloped. It helped to give him resource.

I'm not very impressed by the routines some coaches dream up, in which an enormous class of children swing the racket to music. Nor do I think much of practising your strokes without a ball. I always reckon a child tends to be bored by these things, and I am certain that what the child really wants from the game is the thrill of hitting the ball back and forth.

There is one fundamental rule: the younger the child is when he starts, the easier tennis should be for him. But if your ten- or eleven-year-old has a coach who tries to teach him the American Twist service, change your coach, for this is too advanced for a child of that age.

Once you take the pleasure out of tennis for a youngster, he is lost to the game. You have to make coaching fun for your pupils—coax and kid to them, use a little psychology. But you must never wear them out, or make coaching sessions dull. Advice given in coaching must be easy to comprehend, for, however correct complicated detail may be, it will prove too difficult for most youngsters to follow. The simple fundamentals of the game should be consistently repeated to children without any padding or embroidery.

A helping hand from father Neale Fraser. ▶

Frank Sedgman gives advice to his eldest daughter. ▼

3 YOU MUST HAVE GOOD EQUIPMENT

Ken McGregor

He was a first-class athlete who excelled at Australian Rules football, but concentrated on tennis because his father rightly believed there was a bigger future in this sport than in football. Ken McGregor, born in Adelaide on 2 June 1929, played a vital role in Australia's first post-war Davis Cup win, surprising the American holders by whipping Ted Schroeder in straight sets in 1950. He formed a great doubles partnership with Frank Sedgman. In 1951, they were Australian, French, Wimbledon and U.S. doubles champions, and in 1952, Australian, French and Wimbledon title-holders. McGregor had great height and reach, which enabled him to develop a service and volley game that only the best passing shots could bring undone. Coupled with this, he was a tremendous fighter, chasing every ball to the final point. He was Australia's No 2 singles player to Sedgman in 1950 and 1952 Davis Cup matches. He was runner-up in the Australian Singles to Sedgman in 1950, and in 1951 to Savitt. He won the 1952 title by beating Savitt in the semi-finals and Sedgman in the final. McGregor turned professional after beating Trabert in the 1952 challenge round, returned to football and despite knee-trouble won selection for his State. Today, he runs a sports-store and squash-courts in Adelaide.

An ill-fitting pair of sand-shoes could have prevented my becoming an international tennis player. That may seem an astounding statement, but let me explain . . .

A couple of days before the 1950 Australian championships were to start at Kooyong, I had foot trouble. The sand-shoes I had been wearing at practice were too tight and rubbed the skin from my toes. The toes became infected and I had to visit a doctor to have them lanced. I played in that tournament in an old but comfortable pair of sand-shoes, comfortable only because I had cut parts of the canvas away to take the pressure off my toes. Although unseeded that year, I reached the final, where I was beaten by Frank Sedgman. But my performances in that tournament earned me a place in the 1950 Australian Davis Cup team to go overseas. I often look back and wonder what might have happened had I been forced to withdraw because of sore feet. Some other youngster might have won a place in the Australian touring team, and I could have been struggling to make a name in the following season.

So make sure your shoes fit properly. Take care when buying shoes that they are the correct size—neither too tight nor too sloppy. Walk in them, jump up and down, bend your legs. Then if you are convinced that they are comfortable, buy them.

It is advisable to wear a ribbed sole, which gives a good footing on any surface. The manufacturers nowadays help you by providing special inner soles to prevent

Bob Hewitt, the Australian who now plays for South Africa, presents a fine study in concentration as he waits for a rally to begin in a White City doubles match. Like most leading players he wears a sweat band on the wrist of his racket hand.

jarring as you run about the court. Examine the shoes carefully before you decide on a pair. Once you are in a match and you suddenly develop a blister or sore feet, it is too late. Young French giant Jean Noel Grinda found that out in a tournament in Sydney some years ago when he was playing Don Candy. He had a handy lead, but because of badly fitting shoes his feet began to trouble him. He finished that match in bare feet and with big blisters. Let that serve as a warning. Carelessness can be costly.

Socks play a big part in protecting your feet. I prefer thick or woollen socks which fill out your shoes. Be careful of socks of thin texture or socks that are worn. They tend to rub and chafe your feet. Some players wear two pairs as a safeguard, especially on wooden surfaces which are particularly hard on the feet.

Former South African champion Eric Sturgess was one top-liner who often had trouble with his feet. American ever-green Gardnar Mulloy was another. Both taped the balls of their feet before going out to play a match.

These days, almost every player in a tennis tournament competes in shorts. The days of long trousers for male tennis players have gone forever, it seems. Make sure your shorts fit well, as hitching them up after every rally can ruin your concentration.

I am no expert on women's fashions, but I think girls who go on to the court wearing expensive 'frillies' create a handicap for themselves if their main interest is winning their match. I have always found that the best women players wear neat, well-fitting clothes and never let what they wear interfere with their tennis.

Hair which flops over the eyes frequently is an unnecessary worry to young players, a distraction that breaks concentration. So ensure that your hair is cut so

that this won't occur, or that your hair is kept in place by a ribbon, cap or bandeau.

Children repeatedly ask me whether they should wear sweat-bands, and if so, whether they need them on both wrists. The answer is that you need them if, as most players do, you find perspiration running down your fore-arms into the hands, making the racket wet and difficult to grip. You need them on your free hand only if you perspire so much that you consider the toss-up on service is being hindered.

To all players, the correct choice of a racket is vital. Nothing hinders those seeking to learn the game more than a poor racket. I have often noticed boys and girls who are obviously just starting to play the game, using a racket that is too heavy and has too big a grip. Parents generally are to blame. They hand down their old rackets to their children, and in doing so unwittingly encourage bad habits. Youngsters often find that the only way they can use Dad's racket is to hold it half-way up the handle. Others are forced to use two hands to hit the ball because they haven't the strength to swing freely with one hand. I guess it is only natural for parents to be cautious before outlaying money on a racket for Junior. They are not sure if he will retain his interest in the game. But the best

way to kill his interest is to load him with a 'blunderbuss' racket that is far too big for him to wield freely.

From the start, a child must have a racket that suits his build and the size of his hand. Correct weight and grip are essential. Today manufacturers are producing junior models—rackets that are shorter, lighter and with a smaller grip than the full-size models. As a child's strength develops, he requires a senior model, determined not by his age, but by his rate of growth. Frequently a parent comes into my sports-store and asks for a racket 'to suit a boy aged twelve'. My immediate reply is, 'How big is he, not how old?'

Each individual, whether he is a schoolboy or a seasoned player, should select his own racket. Only he can 'feel' the racket that suits him best. He can be guided by a salesman, but only by handling a racket and swinging it about will he be able to determine the correct balance.

How important is the grip? Well, in 1946, just before Wimbledon, a young American named Jack Kramer was experimenting with rackets, and grips. A blister developed on the palm of his right hand, and plagued him early in the tournament. To combat the discomfort he played in a glove, but by doing so he lost the 'feel' of his racket. Kramer was obviously the best player at Wimbledon that

Roy Emerson at full stretch reaching for a forehand volley knows that his equipment will withstand all the stress of a tough match. Years of research have gone into everything from racket strings to ball pressures.

As Ken McGregor bends to demonstrate a forehand volley, he also demonstrates the value of a racket of weight and handle thickness he can control, and the good impression freshly-laundered clothes make.

Malcolm Anderson demonstrating a backhand volley from close to the net. Australian tennis equipment is rated the world's best by the majority of top-class players.

Now to the question of stringing or tension. John Bromwich used a loosely-strung racket, on the theory that it provided greater control. In his opinion, the ball stayed on the racket a little longer. Well, he certainly had the control to back that statement up! Lew Hoad has a vastly different style from 'Brom'—he is a disciple of the power school—but he likes his rackets strung medium-tight. I liked a racket board-tight. My control was not always good, so I relied on power and placement. From these statements, you have probably deduced a 'rule': tightly-strung rackets for power players, less tension for those relying on control. Well, really there is no rule. Few players in the world possess Ken Rosewall's touch and control, but he likes a tightly-strung racket! Vic Seixas was another 'exception' for he had his rackets strung board-tight. So, you see, it gets back to an individual problem. What suits one person doesn't suit another.

For boys or girls just starting tennis and for the week-end player, the choice of gut or nylon strings is optional. Financially nylon may prove better, for it wears well. In America, a fair amount of synthetic gut is used, but leading players throughout the world prefer animal gut. You don't get the same resilience from synthetic gut. If you don't hit the ball perfectly, the 'feel' is missing. Nylon is used in most junior models—young players don't 'feel' the ball anyway—but as your standard of play improves and a new racket is needed, I recommend the use of animal gut in preference to nylon.

Tennis balls vary around the world. The Italian-made ball, for instance, has low compression, is soft and is terribly hard to hit for a winner. At Wimbledon, balls are kept in refrigerated ice-boxes beside the court to maintain the correct temperature. This way, they at least play normally for part of a match, but they still tend to 'fly' if the weather is hot. A few years ago, balls were changed only at the end of each set at Wimbledon. In 1950, Frank Sedgman and I battled for sixty games before losing a set 31–29 to Americans Tony Trabert and Budge Patty. You can imagine how light those balls were at the end of the sixty games! I think it was in the following year that the rule was altered to allow balls to be changed after so many games.

The type of cloth used on a ball can provide varying effects. The finer cloth doesn't pick up as much grass, and so the balls remain fast. But there are other balls that are fluffy from the outset. Small lawn clippings tend to stick to this cloth, with the result that the ball becomes heavier. The rules provide that balls for match-play when dropped from a height of one hundred inches should bounce to a height of no more than fifty-eight inches and no less than fifty-three inches.

year, but he was eliminated by Jaroslav Drobny in five sets. I think it is fair to say that a faulty grip cost Kramer the 1946 Wimbledon title—even Drobny agreed to that—but he made amends in 1947 when he dominated the men's singles. That year he lost only thirty-one games in nineteen sets.

It's surprising the number of lads who want to use a heavy racket because they think that the bigger the racket the harder they can hit. This is a fallacy. Pancho Gonzales certainly clouted the ball, and yet he usually used a normal $13\frac{1}{2}$ ounce racket with about a $4\frac{1}{2}$ inch grip. For a player of Gonzales's calibre and power, that racket was light.

I used a 15-ounce racket with a 5-inch grip; Don Budge preferred a 16-ounce 'weapon' with no leather grip. That was exceptional, but Budge was a big fellow and he just liked the feel of a racket of that weight. Most leading players use a racket that is heavier than normal and with a slightly bigger grip, but only because they play every day. The ordinary club player, and youngsters, are asking for trouble, in the form of 'tennis-elbow', by trying to use too big a racket.

Peruvian-born Alex Olmedo in action in the 1958 Davis Cup Challenge Round against Australia and Brisbane. Olmedo wore spiked shoes for much of the play and helped the US snatch an unexpected Cup victory.

4 HOLD THE RACKET THIS WAY

Geoff Brown

Wartime Europe was still picking itself up from the rubble in 1946 when a 22-year-old ex-airman with a two-fisted attack happened on to the Centre Court for the first post-war Wimbledon final. His name was Geoff Brown. Appropriately, his opponent was also an ex-serviceman and an ex-prisoner of war, Yvon Petra, of France. Brown was a power player of frail physique and now he tried to pace himself by soft-balling. Petra ran to a two-sets-to-love lead before Brown started to hammer the ball. Brown won the third and fourth sets, and seemed, in the fifth, to have the title won. Match-ball was in sight and Brown middled a deadly two-hander which the baffled Petra, half in jest, played back between his legs for a winner! Brown's confidence was shattered, and Petra went into the record as champion. Brown, who is now a successful Melbourne estate agent, went on to play in another four Wimbledon finals —all doubles—before 1950. A successful two-hander with a cannonball service that his idol, John Bromwich, could have used, Brown tells of the 'how' and 'why' of grips with rare insight, for he has seen or tried them all.

Jack Crawford was asked once what kind of grip he favoured: Did he prefer the Eastern to the Western? Or perhaps he liked the Continental? In the way that was characteristic of his wonderful, natural approach to tennis, 'Craw' replied, 'Well, er, I don't really know what you'd call my grip. But look, if you've got a racket handy I'll show you . . .'

No doubt there are purists who are horrified at such attitudes to the game. But in fact, Crawford gave practical emphasis to the theory that a player should use the grip most comfortable—and suitable—to his type of play. It is a fact that there are basic grips in tennis, just as there are in golf, bowls, cricket, baseball and so on. I am not prepared to advocate rigid adherence to one at the expense of another, since my own experience has convinced me that the basic grips must be regarded as adaptable.

But before explaining my own two-handed stroke and those of erstwhile opponents, I shall summarize the basic grips:

EASTERN: The racket is grasped as one would shake hands. The racket head becomes a virtual extension of the palm of the hand for the forehand stroke. For the backhand, Easterners move the fingers about a quarter-turn around towards the 'top' of the handle. The Easterner can thus play the ball with a flat stroke or he can impart top-spin by rolling the racket over the ball slightly at the moment of contact.

Rod Laver's grip in playing his left-hander's forehand has the same V of the thumb and forefinger pointing straight down the handle.

WESTERN: The racket handle is moved a quarter-turn to the left from that of the Eastern forehand. This gives an ability to hit a higher-bouncing ball—say, at waist-height or higher—with speed, top-spin and relatively superior control.

ENGLISH OR CONTINENTAL: The wrist is kept fairly stiff on the backhand (the forehand is Eastern Style) and the backhand as a result becomes more of a touch-shot.

Coaches have universally expounded these basic grips. Yet one can go to a championship and somewhere see a player who is winning almost in defiance of the teachings of the game. Italy's Guiseppe ('Beppi') Merlo or the Ecuadorian professional Francisco ('Pancho') Segura exemplified this, Merlo with his shortened grasp of the handle of a racket that some opponent once snorted was 'an onion bag', Segura with his two-handed ability to fool even great players about the direction of his shot.

The professionals made Segura's unorthodox game a draw-card, but for my money, the greatest two-handed shot yet seen belonged to Vivian McGrath. I experienced McGrath's game in his declining years as a champion; yet the experience has proved unforgettable. I would class McGrath's two-handed stroke on the left-hand side ahead of the Donald Budge backhand, which is next. McGrath applied his two-hander to the ball very early, always making the stroke as the ball was rising. Fast services made little difference, largely because of his amazing control. He could hit the ball hard, and yet he could angle or lob with equal success. One of his greatest assets was an ability to roll the shot, or to play the lob with almost the same action.

Normal right-handers are inclined to 'telegraph' a lob, even if only slightly, but in the heat of a match it was usually impossible to spot whether Vivian was about to paste up the lines or open up the court. McGrath's forehand was a little weak, but he volleyed well and, like most players using two hands to grip a racket, he was a fine doubles player.

John Bromwich was in the McGrath tradition in that he had a game built around a two-handed grip. But while McGrath was amazing with the two hander on the left-hand side, Bromwich displayed unequalled all-round control. He could do more with a ball than could be imagined, largely because of added attributes of fine anticipation and the ability to sum up an opponent's weaknesses.

Before the war his two-handed shot was flat and reasonably firm, but after the war his game changed and his two-hander never produced the results of six years earlier. At times, post-war, he was inclined to undercut

the two-hander which robbed it of the speed that was always part of its trade mark. This coupled with the fact that his left-handed stroke became the most consistent part of his play, to my mind upset a game based on a natural, two-handed foundation.

It's interesting to observe that Bromwich had to play his ground-strokes well to make up for his weak service. The ball always came back when he served. Taking all these things into account, however, no two-handed player has ever gone as close to winning the world championship as did Bromwich against Falkenburg—three match points in the fifth set of the 1948 Wimbledon final!

The Bromwich two-hander stemmed from an inability at the age of seven to swing a heavy racket properly with

Margaret Court's excellent grip as she bends low for a wide backhand volley is something every aspiring youngster should emulate. The position of forefinger knuckle is noteworthy.

Ken Rosewall demonstrates his forehand grip, with the V formed by the thumb and forefinger pointing straight down the handle.

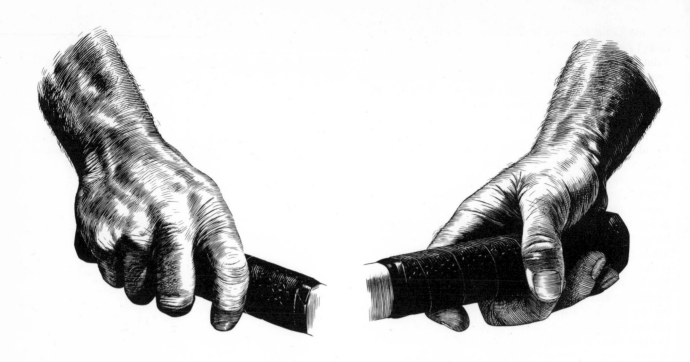

The backhand grip used by most of today's right-handed stars is about a quarter of a turn round the handle from the Eastern forehand position.

The correct grip for right-handers using the widely adopted Eastern forehand. The forefinger is spread well out and behind the racket.

Bob Hewitt demonstrates the hammer grip used by Pancho Gonzales. All the fingers are clenched instead of being spread out as in the Eastern forehand grip. The grip has worked well for Gonzales but is not generally recommended.

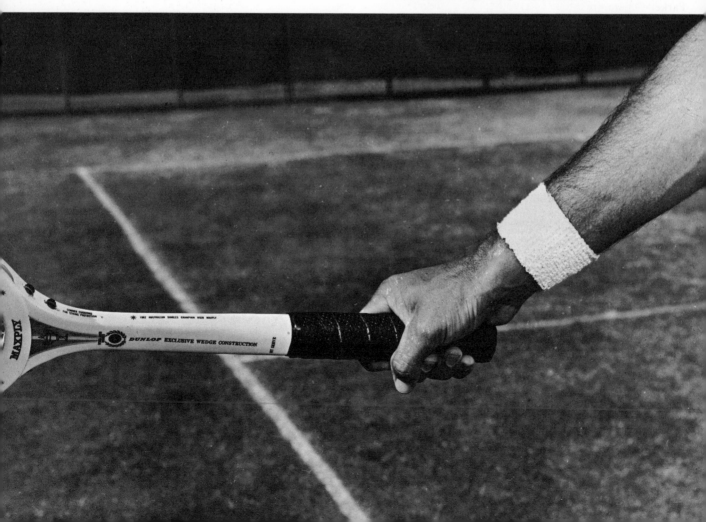

the one hand. Segura's had the same origin. In my own case, I put it down to the fact that at home we were in the habit of continuing our schoolboy cricket on the tennis-court, using a racket as a cricket-bat. I would square-cut, on-drive or hook. When it came to tennis, the two hands naturally stayed on the racket handle!

This created a subsequent problem of what to do on the left-hand side. I tried a two-handed backhand, but found the awkwardness and shortened reach too great a handicap. I also found that I was in trouble playing a normal right-hander's backhand because of the short grip on the two-handed side. After playing an Australian championships quarter-final doubles against Bromwich in Sydney at the ripe age of fifteen, I discussed my back-hand difficulty with him. John suggested that his own left-handed stroke could also solve my problem. I talked it over with my coach, Jim Willard, and we decided to give it a go. When I first played with the left hand I often missed connecting; but I kept at it with a bucket of balls, and by the time I was seventeen, I was hitting with the left hand reasonably well. But I never really had a chance to capitalize on my discovery because the war came six months later—I joined the R.A.A.F. and said goodbye to tennis for nearly four years. I'm sure that, had I been able to continue practising with the left-hand shot, I would have lifted my whole game. I won't argue, how-ever, with those who might claim that the left-hander was my obvious weakness.

The two-handed stroke really comes into its own in doubles. As I have already indicated, there have been some strong combinations employing a two-handed shot —McGrath–Crawford, Bromwich–Quist and Frank Parker–Segura are a few. I have also seen Bob Howe lift a doubles partnership to great heights with his two-hander.

The two-handed player's short back-swing makes for accuracy—the margin for error in the swing is lessened considerably when it is short. (The 'short-swing' tech-nique is now being applied in golf, for the same reason, with marked success.) Also, the strong two-handed grip keeps the racket stable. A fast service to a two-hander has much less chance of dislodging the racket on impact. I invariably stood five feet inside the baseline against Falkenburg's service in doubles (though only in doubles!). This tactic keeps the server under constant pressure—intimidatory pressure if you like. I can recommend it, with the proviso that the two-hander must never move in on the fast service unless he is prepared to watch the ball from the very moment it leaves the server's hand. This is imperative.

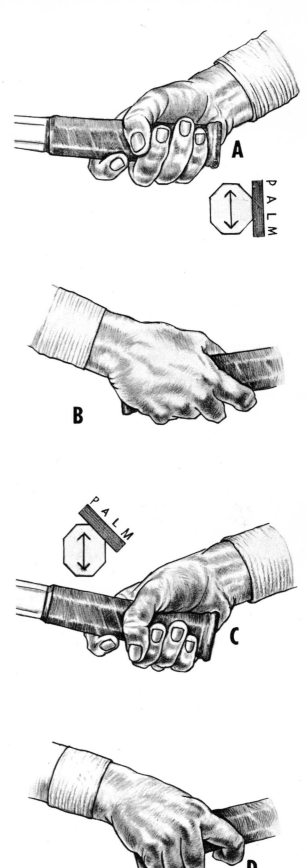

THE BASIC GRIPS

The wrist for the Eastern forehand grip (A) is behind the racket, index finger spread forward. For the Eastern backhand (B), the wrist moves slightly towards the top of the handle. For the Continental forehand (C) the grip is very close to the Eastern forehand grip, but for the Continental backhand (D) the grip moves on top and behind the racket.

5 SERVICE SECRETS
Frank Sedgman

He was born in the Melbourne suburb of Mont Albert on 29 October 1927, son of a tennis club secretary. At twelve, Harry Hopman spotted him chasing every ball in a schoolboy match and invited him to an after-school coaching-class where they developed a power game that was a revolutionary change from the Australian tradition of great base-liners. Sedgman was one of those whose formative years were lost to the war, but he compensated for it by the way in which he worked in the gymnasium and on the court. In 1945 this dedication earned him the Victorian junior title. He missed selection in the 1948 Australian overseas touring team, despite strong objections from Hopman, but went to Wimbledon under his own power, and there, at twenty, won the doubles with Bromwich. In the next four years, he led the drive which took Australia to world supremacy in tennis, taking on the first overseas exponents at their own power game and soundly whipping them. By 1952 he was the greatest amateur of his time, a bright, fresh-faced figure Prime Minister Robert Menzies described as 'one of the most complete champions any game has ever produced'. Sedgman became synonymous with good behaviour, the model coaches urged their pupils to copy on the court. He won every major amateur title, and, with Ken McGregor, formed a superlative doubles partnership that took them to every important doubles crown. He turned professional in January 1953, after having lost only three of the twenty-nine matches he played for Australia in Davis Cup. His aggressive game depended largely on his booming, beautifully produced service.

The service is the most vital stroke in modern tennis. With a powerful service you can defeat an opponent without giving him the opportunity of showing his ground-strokes. If your service is too much for him you completely negate his other shots.

In tennis at all levels, there is always the possibility of hearing 'fifteen-love' called against you before you have had the chance to make a single stroke. In my first visit to Wimbledon in 1948, six-foot-four-inch Bob Falkenburg allowed me such a brief introduction to the Centre Court that he vividly taught me the importance of service power. Falkenburg won Wimbledon that year on service excellence—he had hardly a ground-stroke to his name. In the final against John Bromwich, he won the last game with four terrific services, only two of which Bromwich touched, and all of which Bromwich failed to get back.

Neale Fraser was another Wimbledon winner who owed everything to his service swing. Neale would be the first to agree his ground-shots were poor. Lew Hoad, a fine server himself, thought so much of Fraser's service that he often said nobody ever would have beaten him had he owned Neale's serve.

In deciding at the outset of your tennis career that you must develop a powerful service, keep one factor in mind: the service delivery you end up with must not weaken you so much that it leaves you without fire for other shots or makes you an easy victim in the fifth set. Try to cultivate

an easy, graceful service swing. It's no good being able to hammer them down if the effort reduces you to a physical wreck. Give your service swing rhythm.

THE GRIP: The grip for service and for overhead shots should be the same, as there is little basic difference in how the shots are hit. I use the Continental grip in serving, but the most popular grip among the best players of today is the Eastern. They adopt an Eastern grip half way between the forehand and backhand, with the V-shaped opening formed by the thumb and index finger slightly to the left of centre.

THE TOSS-UP: The action which flips the ball up so that it can be hit, is sadly neglected by beginners. Most of them throw the ball up at varying heights with lackadaisical actions, not stopping to think that this is an absolutely crucial aspect of the serve. So learn a grooved toss-up, with the ball rising under your control as if on a string. Toss at your swing rather than swing at your toss-up. This means you begin your back-swing at the same time as the toss-up. Later, you will learn to vary your toss-up to produce different types of serves, but, for a start, drill yourself to throw it straight up so that it hangs at the top of its rise for you to hit.

BODY POSITION: Your left foot—if you are right-handed—should be three to five inches behind the base-line. Hold the racket in front, with the fingers of the free hand supporting it. Face the right side-line, body perpendicular, shoulder in line with the intended delivery. Your feet should be fifteen to eighteen inches apart.

THE SERVICE SWING: Swing your weight back on to the right leg as you begin the back-swing. The left hand, which steadied the racket in the ready-to-serve position, now moves up to execute the toss-up.

Neale Fraser, who had one of the finest services in postwar tennis, shows the intense concentration he brought to the shot. Fraser is concentrating only on the ball—not where he will hit it.

Toss the ball slightly in front of your body and raise yourself as high as possible on the toes so that the ball moves down into your opponent's court from the highest angle possible. The ball should be hit at maximum height but you must not make the mistake of over-stretching. Your body-weight starts to swing back on to the right leg as the racket moves back and up towards the ball. Keep your eye so intently on the ball that you see the strings make contact with it. As you hit the ball, the left knee is straight. After contact, the racket follows through and down across the left-hand side of your body.

The most successful servers are those who produce such a wide variety of services their opponents are kept guessing. But, whatever the type of service you intend to send down, it must be based on good length, change of direction or pace, swerve or spin. And to achieve these you must master the three basic types of service—the slice, the flat service and the kick service or American Twist.

THE SLICE SERVICE: Side-spin is imparted to this delivery by slicing the racket-head around the outside of the ball, hitting across the right-hand side of the ball as well as the normal motion of hitting down. For the slice, you throw the ball slightly to the right of your body and in front of your head. You bring the racket down and across the body with your racket-arm slightly bent. The slice is usually a second service, for you have to sacrifice speed for accuracy. The trick with the slice is that it breaks

to the receiver's forehand on contact with the ground because of the side-spin on the ball.

THE FLAT SERVICE: This is the shot Falkenburg won Wimbledon with—the cannonball. There is absolutely no spin on the ball, and it flashes straight through after hitting the ground. You brush the slice, but the flat service you strike with an open-faced racket, the strings smacking head-on into the ball. You follow-through down the left side of the body the same as with the slice.

The flat service is achieved with the basic service swing, but it is difficult to control. It is a very effective service on grass or any fast surface, but on clay or a surface that slows the ball when it bounces, flat services lose a lot of their speed.

The Hoad service step-by step. He positions his feet outside the baseline, completes a grooved toss-up, takes his body weight back and then forward into and through the ball. His body-weight swings forward as the racket moves into the ball and he follows through well after contact, sustaining concentration throughout the shot.

Coaching youngsters in Melbourne, I find that those who cannot get the hang of the flat service usually take their eye off the ball on impact, or fail to hit through it. One good way of getting them to continue with the swing on impact, instead of pulling back on the racket, is to

give them an old racket-frame and tell them to throw it in the direction of their rival's service-court from a point as high over their head as they can reach comfortably.

THE KICK SERVICE (AMERICAN TWIST): Throw the ball up a little to your left and just behind your head. Arch your back on the back-swing so that the racket-head approaches the ball from outside and to the left of the ball. The racket connects with a snap of the wrist cutting across and over the ball. This time, you follow through on the same side of the body as your racket-arm, instead of following-through across the body as you do with the flat and sliced serves.

The effect of the kick service is the opposite to the slice, with the ball breaking towards your opponent's backhand. The ball keeps low when you slice it, but, with practice, you can get it to kick quite suddenly and fairly high. Another point is that the ball tends to bounce slowly as well as high, and this may surprise your rival into error.

It takes time to learn to serve well. Few players hit the shot in the same way. But all of them take careful note of where their opponent is standing before they decide which serve to give them. Always hit the ball into the service-court where it will surprise him most. Try not to 'telegraph' your variations in services.

Make it part of your service routine to check where you are standing as you hit the service and you should never have any trouble with foot-faults. The new foot-fault rule—discussed in Cliff Sproule's chapter on rules—should prevent any trouble with foot-faulting, as the rule is far simpler than it has ever been before. The main problem with youngsters who foot-fault is that they forget to check their position and unknowingly drift into the playing-area.

At the start, work on developing a smooth service-swing. Never be satisfied with the service which simply gets the ball into play. Do not try to hit the ball like Hoad or Gonzales too soon; power will come later when your swing is grooved. A strong fore-arm helps get leverage on the ball as you hit it, but the main thing is to pivot so that you get your full body-weight into it.

Hold your service and nobody can beat you. Half the points in this game give you an opportunity to gain an advantage. By regular practice you can accept that advantage.

SERVICE FOOTWORK

(1) John Newcombe lines up his feet so that a line from toe to toe points to the court in which he plans to land the ball.

(2) Newcombe's weight swings on to his left toe as he lifts his right foot. The heels don't touch the turf.

(3) Newcombe's right foot swings forward into court after contact. Even before follow-through ends he is moving forward to the net.

An exercise to help improve the efficiency of your toss up for serving. If the ball falls anywhere in the white area, it's a good ▶ toss-up.

6 ATTACK ON THE FOREHAND

Jack Crawford

John Herbert Crawford came from a country town, Urangeline, in southern New South Wales, and the first net he ever hit a tennis ball over was made of the twine farmers used to bind sheaves of wheat. He has travelled far since those beginnings on a rough-hewn country court, has met kings and queens, tycoons and celluloid idols, but it remains true that he has not spoken ill of any man. That's why they call him 'Gentleman Jack'. He has won all the major honours tennis can bestow, has collected a tax-free testimonial of more than £13,000, been hailed the hero of Wimbledon's greatest final, and he remains the man always mentioned when afficionados seek examples of guile-thwarting, blasting power. He won the 1933 Wimbledon singles complete with buttoned shirt-sleeves, long trousers and square-topped racket, in one of the few spells he ever had overseas in which his asthma was not nightly painful. Crawford was Australian junior champion from 1926 to 1929, won the Australian singles four times, the Australian doubles four times, the New South Wales singles six times, the Victorian singles six times, the French, Wimbledon and German doubles, and played in nine Australian Davis Cup teams. Much of this he achieved because of a superlative forehand, which fooled even players like Harry Hopman. This was one of tennis's great strokes, and no man is better fitted to describe the arts of playing a forehand.

The forehand is the first tennis shot anyone plays, and it is generally the first stroke that is mastered. Unfortunately, this often leads to young players neglecting other departments of the game, for how often we see a player run round his backhand in order to take advantage of his stronger forehand! And this practice is not restricted to novices either.

There is no doubt that everyone should aim to develop an all-court game. But most players who have reached the top have been predominantly forehand players. There are notable exceptions, of course. Ken Rosewall is one of the first to come to mind. However, the strength of a player's forehand is generally an accurate gauge of the all-round strength of his game.

The best forehand I ever saw belonged to Englishman Fred Perry, and he allied this to a brilliant all-court game. Perry perfected the forehand drive, and it became his major match-winning shot. The great American Bill Tilden, was another to master this stroke. Tilden had tremendous power and Perry wonderful accuracy, but the point is that their forehands were unfailingly effective. They created a mental hurdle for all their opponents.

Probably the hardest hitter of the forehand drive in those pre-war days was William ('Little Billy') Johnston, who, with Tilden, formed an almost unbeatable Davis Cup combination for many years. 'Little Billy' was only a handful, but he had a crashing forehand sweep. He was

Roy Emerson's grip is admirably firm as he stretches for a low forehand. He has taken his eyes off the ball but the firm grip ensures an efficient return.

the last world-class player I can remember to use the Western grip, in which the racket is held with the knuckles pointing directly forward, and the palm of the hand facing up. This grip allowed 'Little Billy' to punch the ball with the full face of the racket, and punch it he certainly did. It was particularly useful in dealing with high balls and kicking serves.

Since those days, the Eastern or American grip, popularized by Tilden, has become universal. With this one, often described as the handshake grip, the racket becomes an extension of the forearm, the strings becoming rather like a huge hand. The better a player becomes, the more handle he will use on his forehand to get more power on the ball.

Here are the fundamentals of the forehand drive:

With the Eastern or American grip, both the forehand and the backhand should be played with the racket-handle as nearly as possible parallel to the ground; that is, the wrist should remain level with the centre of the racket wherever the shot is played from, be it ankle, or shoulder-high.

The forehand should always be played by moving in to the ball. At the moment of impact, body-weight should be transferred from the right to the left foot (for a right-hander), so that the full weight of the body can be put behind the ball. The worst mistake you can make in playing a forehand is to back-pedal at the moment of impact. The shot should never be played off the back foot. As in golf, the ball should be hit when it is approximately level with the left heel.

Probably the most underestimated advice ever given to players is that which is most flagrantly disregarded:

RACKET HEAD ON BALL

CHOP

UNDERCUT

SLICE

TOPSPIN

Wrist strength and flexibility is vital in achieving the full range of forehand shots. Some players develop this strength by squeezing a squash ball in the palm of their hand.

Keep your eye on the ball right on to the racket. And this is especially true when youngsters play their forehands.

The most important point of any shot is that it be effective, whatever your method of playing it. It doesn't matter how hard or stylishly a ball is hit; if it doesn't win points, it's not good enough.

I found the most effective way of hitting a forehand was to take it on the rise—that is, hit it as soon as possible after the bounce without making it into a half-volley. As far as I can remember, this method of playing a forehand was introduced by Sir Norman Brookes, and no one can argue with the results he achieved with it. I have always contended that if you can take a ball eighteen inches earlier than the average player you have gained a yard on the chap at the other side of the net. I was often criticized for playing my forehand this way. My critics said I would play a better shot if I stood back a little and gave myself more time. But you can't have it both ways.

Admittedly, there is more room for error when taking the ball early. But by taking the ball early you are in a much better position to take the opposition unawares and get into an attacking position. By standing inside the base-line to receive service, you can often unsettle the server by getting the ball back to him before he has time to get to the net. The shot hit on the rise doesn't have to be as good as the one hit late, as it has the advantage of surprise.

By taking the ball early, the player has a better opportunity to hit the ball at the height he wants it, particularly in the return of service. The closer to the bounce the ball is taken, the less variation there will be in its height, which can be affected by such things as the amount of spin on the ball and the condition of the court surface. If a kicking service can't be taken on the rise, the player will often have to wait for it to come down, which allows the server all the time in the world to position himself for the return.

Pancho Segura, the tiny two-handed freak from Ecuador, perfected the quick return of service. At some time or another, he has been able to bustle all the top pros. by banging their services back on the rise. This can rattle even the best servers in the game. It forces them to try to hit the ball just a bit harder, and inevitably errors creep in.

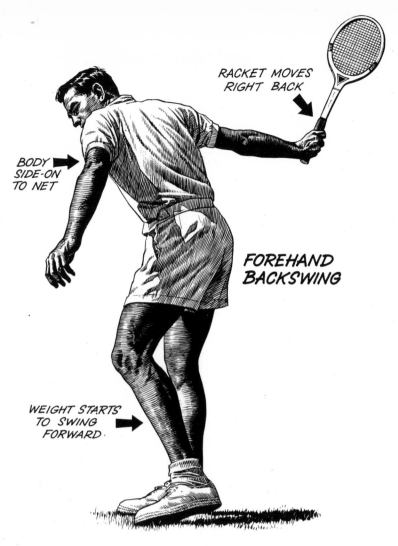

RACKET MOVES
RIGHT BACK

BODY
SIDE-ON
TO NET

FOREHAND
BACKSWING

WEIGHT STARTS
TO SWING
FORWARD

A strong forehand drive stems from taking a full swing at the ball and by transferring your body weight back and then forward into the stroke.

Personally, I have always found the flat forehand the most effective. I don't believe there is anything to be gained by trying to spin the ball in singles play, though in doubles there is often a case for using top-spin to get the ball to drop over the net as soon as possible and thus make volleying more difficult.

But I have always considered that the more spin there is on a ball the less likely it is to be an effective shot, particularly in top-class tennis.

The flat drive travels faster than the under-cut or over-spun shot and it doesn't bounce as high. Undoubtedly, there is more risk of netting a flat drive, as it usually has to be hit within an inch or two of the net to remain in court. But it is the attacking way of hitting a forehand, and much more likely to result in a winner. The top-spinner usually can be played to clear the net by two feet, as the spin will bring it down into court. But it bounces high, making return easier.

By hitting straight through the ball (flat), the player has much more control of length. You can never know exactly how much spin you have put on the ball, and so you must allow a margin for error. Thus a spinning drive

can never be hit right to the base-line with any real certainty that it will go in. A flat drive is the most penetrating. It is more of an attacking shot than the under-cut forehand or top-spin forehand.

It is extremely difficult to master all three methods of hitting the forehand. Tilden has possibly been the only one to do so in my memory. Hoad probably gets closest among the current players. Hoad hasn't achieved Tilden's perfection, but he has more dash.

Most top-class players today concentrate on the top-spin forehand drive— probably because there is less emphasis today on ground-shots and more on volleys.

Among post-war players, Kramer possibly developed the flat forehand drive better than anyone else. This is undoubtedly the reason why he was so good.

One of the great differences between the amateur and professional today is that the pro. has better mastery of the flat drive.

The ability to conceal the direction of a shot is invaluable to a tennis-player. I've seen many with a good forehand who were never effective because they always 'telegraphed' exactly where the shot was going. This is

35

something which is nearly impossible to teach; it's a matter of reflexes mainly—you've either got it or you haven't. Most players who can conceal the direction of their shots can't explain exactly how they do it. It is done by a quick change of mind almost at the point of impact. The changed direction is then achieved by speeding up or slowing down the racket in the last instant, so as to meet the ball with the face of the racket at an angle.

For instance, take the player who decides on a forehand drive straight down the line. At the last minute, he sees the line covered, so he snaps his racket through faster than planned, and by so doing directs the ball straight across court. It might seem relatively simple to achieve, but the mere fact that so few have mastered the art proves it is not.

The successful double-handed forehand players—Segura, Brown and Bromwich—could all conceal the direction of their shots. But they had the advantage of not needing a long back-lift to get power. When perfected, this double-hander is a most effective shot. As well as enabling a player to conceal direction, it allows him to hit the ball harder and earlier than if he were using the orthodox forehand. I would never advise anyone to change his style if he had a good double-handed forehand. I consider that only Perry and Tilden among the orthodox had better forehands than the double-handers. The only disadvantage of the grip is that a player can't reach as far with it.

The effectiveness of the running forehand often means the difference between good and very good players. Fred Perry had probably the best running forehand of all time. Hoad, Rosewall and Sedgman are also outstanding in this department. The running forehand is one of the first shots to break down under pressure. The important thing is to be on balance at all times, to move on to the ball and to play it confidently. Once again, back-pedalling is a cardinal error.

As with all the shots in the game, there is no substitute for practice, practice and more practice. Aim for accuracy first and you will gradually find your speed-limit.

Confidence is an invaluable quality for a tennis-player. He who goes for his shots—and expects them to go in—usually gets them in. For an example of a lack of confidence, we have only to look at Margaret Court and Wimbledon in 1962. Before and after the championships, she was almost in a class of her own. But at Wimbledon she lost all confidence and played tentatively. Like many other champions, she plays much better when she is hitting the ball hard. If you are used to playing this way—and an attacking style will usually prevail—your game will probably fall apart if you try to play it at a different tempo. The forehand is an attacking shot, and it always should be played that way.

Rod Laver's forehand drive played from the classic position—i.e. with the opposite foot right across. On the backhand side his left foot would stretch across the body and take his weight.

7 HOW TO PRACTISE PROPERLY

Evonne Goolagong

Evonne Fay Goolagong was born in the NSW country town of Barellan on 31 July 1951, of part aborigine parents. Her father works as a shearer and station hand in the town (Population 900). Evonne has four brothers and three sisters. She began playing tennis at the age of seven on the Barellan War Memorial courts and was encouraged by Mr Kurtzman, who helped her compete in small country tournaments and retains a close interest in her progress. In August 1961, coaches Colin Swan and Mrs F. Martin, from the Victor Edwards' Tennis School in Sydney sent Edwards a glowing report on Evonne. 'We think we have found a potential champion,' they said. Edwards went to the clinic and after watching Evonne play—she was then only nine—decided to foster her tennis career. For the next four years Evonne trained at the Edwards' Tennis School in Sydney during school vacations, staying with Edwards and his wife. At the age of fourteen, by arrangement with Mr and Mrs Goolagong, Mr Kurtzman and members of the Barellan Tennis Club the Edwards became Evonne's legal guardians and she went to live permanently at their home. Her progress at school and on the tennis court was outstanding. She graduated from winning age group titles to State junior teams, won two Australian junior hardcourt singles and the Australian junior grasscourt singles. In 1968 she passed the High School Certificate at Willoughby High School, which she represented in swimming, basketball, athletics and tennis. She made her first overseas tour in 1970 and won eight of the twenty-one Open tournaments in which she played, defeating world ranked players such as Kerry Melville, Karen Krantzcke, Judy Dalton, Rosemary Casals, Winnie Shaw and Nell Truman. Back home she showed immediate benefit from the tour, winning the Queensland hardcourt and grasscourt singles, the Australian hardcourt title and playing an important role in Australia's Federation Cup team by beating Francois Durr, of France, and in the final Virginia Wade, of Britain. She followed this with an extraordinary win over world champion Margaret Court in the final of the Victorian singles. In the 1971 Australian singles final she led Mrs Court 5–2 in the third set but lost a stirring match. But Evonne's major triumph came at the 1971 Wimbledon Tennis Championships when she became the women's singles champion by defeating three-times Wimbledon singles winner Margaret Court, 6–4, 6–1 in sixty- three minutes.

The tennis player who does nothing but play matches can never achieve maximum satisfaction from the game or hope to reach the top. For practice, and the business of fashioning a game that will withstand intense pressure on all types of surfaces and under all circumstances is an essential part of lawn tennis. Its no good just playing sets —you must work on stroke production, sharpening of the reflexes and all the other parts of a good player's repertoire.

From my early days as a youngster on the hardcourts of Barellan I have been captivated by tennis. It is not an easy game to master, even for a few games, but it would not be so rewarding and have attracted so many people all over the world if it did not represent such a challenge. So it is wise to decide right at the beginning of your tennis career that you are going to accept that challenge by practising whenever you can.

The majority of today's top players have a coach to whom they can go when faults develop in their game. Usually these are the coaches with whom they started

Hours of hard practise have gone to make the agility Australian Ken Fletcher shows in making this smash at Wimbledon against the Swede Ulf Schmidt.

when their competitive tennis began. Sometimes these coaches can eliminate a fault in just a few minutes, but it is important to remember that the coach cannot guarantee that the fault is permanently fixed. It is up to the player to remember the causes of the fault when they are away from the coach's supervision out on the court. When you have reached open tournament standard, you generally just work on your faults out on the practice court. But years before this, at the stage where you are considered a promising junior, you follow a specially prepared training schedule. This is how we did it at the Vic Edwards tennis school:

PHYSICAL TRAINING: We worked for a set period every day on callisthenics to improve our physiques, exercises designed to build stamina and smarten up our reflexes.

REFLEX TRAINING ON COURT: Working usually in a squad of three or four players we volleyed firstly against one another from short distances, always trying to keep the ball under control. Then we changed to one player on one side of the net against three on the opposite side, the lone player standing up at the net while the other three drove the ball at her from the back of the court. Next the players at the back of the court moved to the net

in turn. There were no rests—we worked all the time—and the players all took turns in volleying against the other three.

STROKE CORRECTION AND PRODUCTION: Again in a squad of four, we rehearsed driving the ball up and down the tramlines. Then we changed to crosscourt driving, and finally to round robin driving or driving crosscourt or down the lines at the coach's command. About 40 minutes of this without a spell soon irons out any problems in your driving.

SERVING: We left this until the training period was well advanced to ensure that we were properly warmed up, but even then we started with slow, easy services. Once we were stroking the services solidly we moved on to hitting them according to a command, serving straight and flat for a time and then swinging the ball to the right or left. While one player spent a strenuous 15 minutes rehearsing services, the others practised their returns of service. Finally when all the serves were working well we played out the first point just to get the server accustomed to moving in behind the serve.

Harry Hopman, with one of his successful Davis Cup teams. All of the players have strong, durable legs, and all have trim waist lines, without any excess weight.

COURT PLAY AND SETS: Only after we had drilled our way through each phase of the game did we get on to playing sets. All the time the coach was watching and instructing us. I am sure that if a coach was not present the practise session could become lax and even a little slovenly and much of the benefits would be lost. Even top players sometimes get into bad habits, such as allowing the ball to bounce twice, when their practice workouts are not supervised.

My coach, Vic Edwards, always says the important thing is to plan your practice. It is not necessary to spend hours every day at it, but it is essential to use the time well. Too many young players want to play sets instead of working on their stroke production or on sharpening their reflexes. This is a big mistake.

I don't like long practice sessions. A solid hour in a sweat-suit is usually enough for me if nothing is badly wrong with my game. If something is wrong then I go on for longer than an hour trying to correct it. But I can't practise for hour after hour like some girls. When the American girls Pattie Hogan and Sharon Walsh stayed with us at the Edwards' Sydney home in the Australian summer of 1970–71, they spent hours every day on Mr Edwards' courts. I couldn't do that.

Even before the Federation Cup matches in Perth just before Christmas 1970, we did not work out for long periods. The practice periods I had with Margaret Court were very solid. We worked hard. But we did not go on for hours until we were bone weary.

As you develop I think it is important not to rely too heavily on your coach. It is comforting to have someone close by who can remind you that you have forgotten to make allowances for the wind or something fundamental like that. But I feel I have been lucky because Vic Edwards has always insisted that I should think for myself. He did not worry me, for example, with special work on my forehand when some sportswriters were saying it was weak early in my first overseas trip in 1970. He let me work out my forehand problems myself, but I guess he must have been relieved when I started to hit the shot fairly well.

One of the fascinating aspects of tennis is that if there is a weakness in a player's game when he or she has reached world ranking that fault will remain. Coaches usually find it impossible to correct a fault once a player has started to compete at Wimbledon. By then it's too late and the player has to live with it, be it a weakness in serving or when the ball is in the air or a failure to hit a certain type of volley. I am told that John Bromwich had a weakness on the smash all his life—but he was considered unlucky not to have won Wimbledon. Other great players had simple pat-ball services.

For the young tennis player, the objective should be, however, to build a game that has no weaknesses, a game in which every stroke is properly produced and every tactical situation is met with a counter. The only reliable way of achieving this is to learn to practise properly right from the start of your tennis career.

Evonne Goolagong has made outstanding progress on the tennis court and is destined for great things.

8 SURFACES FOR ALL TASTES
Mervyn Rose

In 1971 at forty-one, Mervyn Rose was coaching almost daily around Melbourne, a seasoned topline professional. After Sedgman and McGregor turned professional, Rose set his seal on the title of top Australian amateur by winning the 1954 Australian singles championship. He also won the singles championships of France, Italy, Germany, Chile, Sweden and the Argentine, a Wimbledon doubles title and two U.S. doubles crowns—without ever looking properly fit. Until he joined the professional ranks himself in 1959, he spearheaded the Australian left-handers' attack on the world's major amateur tournaments in the 1950s, Neale Fraser, and then Rod Laver, following in his wake. A brilliant interceptionist, Rose was probably the most successful Australian tourist on the post-war European amateur circuit, largely because he was so good on clay or hardcourt surfaces. He was certainly the most colourful Australian at large—from Barranquilla to Bastaad, from Prague to Panama City. Here he explains his winning approach to the slower European game and details all known tennis surfaces.

Whenever anyone starts talking about the different court surfaces in different countries, I call over Pat O'Kane, a longtime farmer friend, and say: 'Pat, tell 'em about the time you played that 45-year-old Czech in Paris.' It's the most entertaining half-hour I know to hear Pat, a Victorian country champion of no mean standing, relate the story of his first major tournament singles on the slow porous back courts of the Roland Garros stadium in Paris.

Pat strode forward at his full six-feet-plus, brimful of confidence, on a glorious Paris-in-the-Springtime morning, to start the match. The crisp air was heavy with the woody scent of the adjacent Boulogne Forest and the powdery red clay looked a picture for a game—especially against a first-round opponent on the wrong side of forty. Yet a couple of hours later, Pat was to slump, beaten, on to a bench in the club-house, a trail of wrecked friendships in his wake.

The experience of Czechoslovakia had turned the tide against the O'Kanes of Katamatite long before Pat had tackled the umpire about scoring in French, which he couldn't understand. Pat's time had run out well before he had decided there was no future in driving hard on a court which robbed the ball of every vestige of speed, long before the loopy-boopy Continental game of his shuffling opposition not only confounded him but churned up the soft surface of the court until it looked like Bondi Beach on Boxing Day. Pat, touring in European tennis for the first time, promised me afterwards that never again would he rebuke me for what he considered

Mervyn Rose in action on grass. On the clay courts of Europe he was far more effective than most Australians, winning a hatful of major championships.

my 'misdemeanours' on court. In his view, European tennis deserved all the so-called 'tantrums' it got—and then some!

What had happened was that a wily opponent had carved up Pat's grass-court game on the slow European clay. Using a racket with slack stringing—this holds the ball on the racket longer for greater control—the Czech lobbed, angled, passed and generally tied up his net-rushing opposition.

Even more confounding was O'Kane's discovery that the en-tout-cas of Paris was totally different from that of Australia. In Australia, the brick-dust is like sugar on concrete. In Europe, it is powdery—all the way down. The result is that the serve-and-volley game holds no terrors for the European trouper. He has all the time in the world to reach the ball. I remember a day in Rome when we sat in the sun and averaged out the rallies between two middle-aged competitors at something like seventy-eight shots. As they stood six feet outside the base-line, it was rally-rally. They played four sets in five hours. This sort of thing allows players to stay in European tournament tennis for years and years. Patty and Drobny used their experience of these conditions to dominate European tennis from 1949 to 1956.

I liked European clay for the reason that, despite statements to the contrary, I have not always been a net-rusher. I didn't rush the net until I was seventeen, and the only reason I did so then was that Sedgman and McGregor were rushing me! When I got to Europe, I found that I could stay back and hack a few. My all-round background thus proved an advantage over the grass-court net-rushers who were on the circuit with me. Laver, in his grand-slam year, said that he found the same thing.

The first things I learned in Europe were about shots that I seldom used, or saw used, in Australia. The grass-court game is so hurried that it is easy to spot the lob or the deep shot. But on slow European clay it is easy to disguise such shots. As a matter of interest, the only players I could say played really successful grass-court lobs were the two-handers—Segura and Bromwich. They say McGrath was even better, but I didn't see him in a championship. The two-handers, with their iron grips, are able to disguise the lob much more easily.

Being a left-hander, I also found that I could exploit my ability to spin and kick my service to the right-hander's backhand. The right-hander usually finds his stronger service is the one that kicks to the opponent's forehand. This, then, meant that I gained even more time to get to the net, and that when I did get there, I was at a volleying advantage.

I also took the hint from the locals and used a racket with about forty-eight to fifty pounds tension compared with about fifty-eight to fifty-nine pounds for grass.

Rod Laver in his younger days practising on a Brisbane hardcourt which enabled him to slide into his shots.

'Beppi' Merlo moulded a mighty successful clay-court game around rackets he used to string himself. He didn't need any gear for the job either—he would just tug away and tie a few loose ends and he was back in the game! Merlo's control with such slack stringing was amazing. John Bromwich had a similar attitude. He'd often pluck the strings, and if the tune wasn't in the key he sought, he'd reckon the racket was too tightly strung!

I will always remember playing Beppi Merlo in the semi-finals of the Rome international at the Foro Italico in 1957. The points seemed to last forever, and you felt that every shot Merlo got back had been fired out of a catapult. Merlo once held up a match against Bob Howe while a ball-boy went to the dressing room and replenished the bags of saw-dust he used to stop his grip slipping. This must have been the only time in history that saw-dust stopped play!

It's an eerie court, that one in Rome. The back walls seem about fifty yards away from the base-lines and they have those big marble statues all around. This gives the effect of playing on a postage-stamp. It's nothing like the tight stadium atmosphere that you get used to year after year at Kooyong, Wimbledon or Roland Garros. You also have a bit of trouble stalling when the heat is on

in Rome. The ball-boys are so far away that they can't hear you call to clear the court!

By way of contrast, the fastest surface I have ever seen is a linoleum court near the Longwood Cricket Club courts at Boston. Sedgman and McGregor were to have played Don Candy and me in the final of the U.S. national doubles in 1951, but the match was rained out. (Sedgman and McGregor later won the postponed final at Forest Hills.) Because of the rain, we moved indoors on to the linoleum for some practice, only to find that the surface was so fast that nobody could return a serve. We were at 32–all when we stopped! I remember at one stage reaching agreement to serve our second service first so that we might at least get a rally going.

Boards would come next for speed, depending of course on the way that they're laid. If sideways, they tend to take more spin. Wembley in London, for example, is a surface laid in wooden squares and you can do a lot more with a service if it hits particular parts of the squares. Canvas over boards or ice is also very fast. At Madison Square Garden, in New York, they use canvas on ice most successfully. Once the fuzz wears off the canvas it really speeds up the game.

Really dry or sunburnt grass would be next in my speed-rating—say Kooyong at Davis Cup time. The grass is shaved almost bare, so that you are playing virtually on dirt with grass clippings on top. It's interesting to note that although the East Coast of the U.S. has grass-courts at the major tennis centres, they are notoriously uneven. This is one reason for the development of the net-rushing game. Players began rushing the net because they daren't let the ball bounce too often. After being feet under snow in the winter, the courts usually have more humps than a camel by the time summer comes along.

The best grass-courts I have played on are the Wimbledon courts at the start of the second week—when they begin to tinge with brown.

But if I were putting down a court, I would go for cement. It's a slower surface than dry grass, but it is the only really true surface. When you have a true, fast bounce, the only problem is with the weather at the time of the match.

You strike some odd surfaces at times, particularly on the faster-moving professional circuit. I toured South Africa with the pros. once and we played twenty-nine matches in twenty-one days. We chartered two planes to fly us around. One day we would play on concrete at sea-level, next day at 6,000 feet on grass, next day on what they call 'ant-juice' (a flaky surface not unlike asphalt in appearance), and then back to sea-level and clay. I remember I had six rackets, two of each tension I thought I might need. The other boys had the same number, though no one was saying much to anybody else on the subject of what tensions they were using. After all, we were playing for money!

My most unforgettable experience in court surfaces is of a cow-dung one at Bombay. There are similar ones throughout India. I stopped over for practice at Bombay one time and tried them out. Different sects have different religious customs in India, and I defy anyone to forget running up against opponents playing in the heat of India on cow-dung—particularly against players of that sect which abhors water for washing, preferring instead a special oil. Several players have confided to me since that they spent a good deal of their time-out on the court seeing to it that they changed ends down the opposite side of the court to that used by their opponents! The court surface sticks to perspiring limbs much as dusty clay. It creeps up your legs as the match goes on. Even when you use water for washing, the odour stays with you for days.

Tennis in the mountains of South America can have its moments, too. I remember gasping for breath at 14,000 feet in La Paz, Bolivia, and deciding to move on without a match. I also recall playing at Bogota, Colombia, at 9,000 feet. The air was so thin that the balls had holes in them to make them manageable. In addition, we devised our own solution to the thin-air problem, playing only five games and then deciding that the losers should play again. The winners really earn their rest-periods up there.

The year I played in the South American circuit was the year that I was involved in three revolutions—in Buenos Aires, Argentina; Caracas, Venezuela, and in Paris. Having weathered the take-over from Farouk by Colonel Neguib in Cairo a few years earlier, it was like old times to walk on to courts through corridors and gates guarded by heavily-armed soldiers. I have vivid memories of the touchy troops around the Caracas stadium. It was the sort of thing that made you think twice about querying a line decision! But that wasn't as unnerving as a later appearance with the pros. in Algiers during the 'Keep-Algeria-French' emergency. There, with people dying in bomb-attacks within hearing distance, we played under the barrel of a machine-gun which covered the court and its surroundings. But that is another story . . .

Robyn Ebbern, a former top-ranking Australian junior, slides into a backhand volley.

9   GET THAT SERVICE BACK
Mal Anderson

Queensland's domination of Australian tennis in the 1950s was largely helped by the skill of a coach named Charlie Hollis, who had two proteges in the Davis Cup team at the same time, Mal Anderson and Rod Laver. Anderson, at his best, was one of the greatest players who ever lived, but his best was fairly elusive. He showed glimpses of it when he had Hoad in difficulties at Wimbledon in 1956, and again in his dazzling 1957 U.S. singles final win over Cooper. For the rest, Malcolm James Anderson, born 3 March 1935, in the Queensland country town of Theodore, has seldom been able to string more than a few games of his best tennis together at one time. But even an out-of-form Anderson has a remarkable return of service. Anderson's long lean legs carry him about the court with remarkable speed, and he is one of the most classic shot-makers in tennis. Seldom has this been better used than in the doubles with Mervyn Rose at the 1957 Melbourne Davis Cup Challenge Round. Anderson was brilliant, his returns of service superfine, and he and Rose swept Seixas and MacKay from the court in three sets, Rose repeatedly hammering away the winners Anderson's returns of service set up. Anderson married Roy Emerson's sister and when he is not making one of his infrequent appearances at professional tournaments—he joined Kramer after the 1958 challenge round at Brisbane—they live in their Brisbane home with their children.

Hold your service in tennis, and nobody can beat you. This catch-phrase, as old as the game itself, is consistently proved in important matches when players with little equipment except a powerful service do well. Thus, the ability to return service well enough to break your opponent's service is a crucial aspect of the game.

Frequently, when spectators are disappointed in a match from which they expected sustained thrills, the players' failure to return service is the cause. This is probably truer today than it was before the war because so much emphasis is now placed on learning a power service. Indeed, against top-liners like Pancho Gonzales, John Newcombe, Arthur Ashe and Rod Laver, you cannot hope to win unless you get their big serves back fairly consistently.

Learning to return service accurately not only worries your opponents but will help improve your ground strokes. Obviously, if you can get fast first services back, you should find the ground-strokes easier, with much slower balls to deal with and more time to get into position.

One of the secrets of returning service consistently well is to adopt the right 'ready' position. My old coach, Charlie Hollis, used to insist that all his pupils adopted this position—and pity the boy or girl who neglected to do so! Charlie was right to place such importance on this, as you have no chance against a really big service unless you can cut to an absolute minimum the preliminaries

Ken Rosewall boasts one of the best returns of service in the business, partly because of his fitness, partly because of his sustained concentration.

needed to get you into position to hit the ball.

In the 'ready' position, you stand with the racket held level with the centre of your body. Hold the butt loosely with your right hand, so that you can quickly use the backhand or forehand grip as required. The throat of the racket should be held in the left hand and it is this hand which does most of the work in thrusting the racket quickly in to place forehand or backhand returns.

The quick adjustment of your grip on either the forehand or backhand side is vital because you just do not have time to change your grip against a really powerful service. I like the hammer grip for returning service, as it allows you to play a backhand or a forehand with comfort and control.

Facing a booming Gonzales-type service, you have an absolute minimum of time to make your shot and the ball itself carries all the pace you require to get it back. Thus, a long back-swing is unnecessary and a waste of important time. You play the return as a block-shot with very little back-swing, but with a follow-through which helps control the direction of your return. The follow-through is important whatever shot you play, but this doubly applies in returning service. You can best make use of the speed your opponent has put on the ball by keeping your wrist absolutely firm on impact. The time factor also limits your foot-work, so try to use what time you have to get your body-weight moving forward into the ball at the instant you make contact.

I believe in changing my grip to receive the second service because the ball comes to you at a far slower speed than the first service. You have more time to select the grip used and you have more time to get your feet into position to play a firm shot. Move in to the ball

Among all the great players around the world Ken Rosewall has one of the best returns of service.

Neale Fraser struggling to control a fierce service return, surprised by the power his opponent applied to returning a strong service.

and get over the ball in the same motion.

These days, almost every class player uses a kicker for his or her second service, with the ball moving away from the receiver and also bouncing higher. That is why good foot-work is essential in returning seconds. You can use a longer back-swing, too, because you do not have so much pace already on the ball and you now have time to make your own speed. It is important to make contact with the ball at the top of its bounce as this gives you more control and a higher margin for error.

I have often been involved in arguments about where you should return service. In my view, you cannot lay down a set rule for this, as it's impossible to make up your mind where the return should go until the service arrives. Against some services, you have no option.

Always take the racket back at the same height as the ball when it is at the top of its bounce, but do not follow through so far that you are off balance for the next shot.

When your returns repeatedly fail, examine these factors for the cause:

- Are you keeping your eye on the ball right up until it strikes the racket strings?
- Are you making your preparations early enough to take the ball in front of the body and not level or behind it? Remember that you should strike the ball six to eight inches in front of your torso on all occasions.
- Is your wrist firm throughout the stroke and particularly on impact? This is where your control comes from.

I have always found Pancho Gonzales's service the most difficult of all the big serves to receive. He always manages to keep you guessing about what kind of serve the next one will be, and where he will place it. Playing Gonzales helps improve your return of service, as you know before you take the court that you just have to get his service back somehow to have even a slight chance of winning.

The fastest service I have received, though, was Lew Hoad's when he was right at his peak. I remember a few

Margaret Court hits with the power of a man and is as fast and mobile as any woman player has ever been.

Ken McGregor's long legs and his exceptional reach get him to a ball others may have missed. Ken, a natural athlete, could cover the court in two strides.

times when I did not even see the balls which whizzed by me, let alone make an attempt to get them back. The vital thing when this happens is not to let it break up your concentration for the next service return. Stay on the job, however many aces the power-servers put down.

The three greatest players I've returned services against are, in order, Gonzales, Hoad and Rosewall, and unless I faithfully followed the rules of returning services I've set down here, my whole game seemed to fall apart against them. Against a really heavy service, you can still have difficulty getting the ball back if you do everything correctly, but you have no chance at all if you forget the 'drill'.

In doubles, you do not usually have the problem of having to take the really powerful speed service, as it's important to get the first service in and most players slow down their first for doubles. But you have less uncovered court into which to hit the ball. It is unnecessary to take a long back-swing in doubles because you must try to drop the ball at the feet of the incoming server, so that he has to volley upwards. This way, you or your partner have a chance to cut off his return or intercept it.

To keep the pressure on your opponents in doubles, you must be moving forward as you return service. This is even more essential in doubles than singles, as you have to play much of a doubles match from the net. This is the dominating position all good doubles players seek, and

you won't get there by hanging back after you return service.

In his chapter of this book, Colin Long explains the great importance returning service has in doubles, and how the great John Bromwich could go through a match without missing a single service return. Bromwich may have been helped with his returns by the added control two hands on the racket gives, and perhaps the loose stringing of his racket enabled him to get more 'purchase' on the ball. But fundamentally he carried out the vital points I have described, and his concentration was nothing short of remarkable.

We may not have reached Bromwich's standard in returning service, but most of us have had our big days when we got most of them back. I remember the day in Melbourne, in Challenge Round doubles with Mervyn Rose, when I set up a lot of points for Rose with good returns which forced Vic Seixas and Barry MacKay to hit the ball up. Rosie was dynamic at the net that day, but it gives me great pleasure that I set them up for him in the same way that Bromwich set them up for Adrian Quist, or Ken McGregor set them up for Frank Sedgman.

And who among all the great players I have seen around the world has the best return of service? My vote goes to Ken Rosewall, who is a model for all aspiring young tennis players to follow if they want to master the tricky but satisfying art of return service.

51

10 THE BACKHAND MYTH
Lew Hoad

Alan and Bonnie Hoad reared three sons in their semi-detached home at Glebe Point, Sydney; Larry, Kelly and Lew. The boys roamed the streets barefoot, played park football, and cricket, and bowled old car-tyres down back lanes with other urchins. The Hoad's were handsome, friendly people who existed on Alan's modest pay for repairing trams for the Transport Commission. Lew was the moody one who disliked school-books and often got into trouble through his casualness. He grew up with a tennis racket seldom far away, and he became one of the best players who ever lived, some say the greatest big-occasion player of all. Lew Hoad, born on 23 November 1934, represented Australia in Davis Cup from 1952 to 1956. With Rosewall, Hoad retained the Cup for Australia when both were nineteen. He won the Wimbledon doubles with Hartwig in 1955, and with Rosewall in 1956, the year he narrowly missed the grand slam of the world's major singles, winning the Australian, French and Wimbledon titles, and losing to Rosewall in the final of the U.S. titles. In 1957, Hoad won Wimbledon for the second year running, overwhelming Cooper in fifty-seven minutes with a dazzling display. Immediately, he turned professional for the biggest guarantee ever paid an amateur sportsman—£280,000. Today he is a rich man with blocks of flats of his own, a share in a hotel, gilt-edge stock investments, a beautiful wife and three handsome children. He has lived in Spain for some years where he is developing a large sporting complex. Recently he returned to big tennis but his tournament play is restricted. As ever, the sign that Hoad is in form remains the sight of his top-spin backhands whipping past opponents closing on the net.

Most people when they start in tennis are scared of the backhand. This fear is nonsensical. The backhand is the most natural shot of them all. So cast all that stuff about its being difficult out of your mind. It's a myth.

The backhand probably has brought me more wins than any other shot, especially in my amateur days, when the first thing a player new to your game tried was to fire a ball down your backhand side.

It's important at the outset to get one fact firmly implanted in your mind about the backhand: the right grip makes the shot easy. With the right grip you can hit backhands back even if your feet are out of position. As tennis is played today, it is difficult to get a grip that is practical for all shots. The best grip is the one that is comfortable to you. If your grip on the backhand feels cramped or in any way awkward, change it.

Most great players play their backhands with an Eastern grip with the wrist slightly behind the racket, about a quarter-turn on the right of the forehand position, for right-handers and a quarter-turn on the left for left-handers. The wrist plays a vital role and should be locked steel-firm at the moment of impact. Keep the thumb pressed firmly against the back of the grip because this will help keep the racket-head steady.

Closer to the net Rosewall plays a low backhand volley, but again with the same careful attention to the ball's flight.

There are three basic backhand shots:

1. The flat backhand in which you hit the ball with the strings flat on impact.

2. The top-spin backhand, in which you start with the racket-head under the ball and roll the strings over the ball on impact.

3. The sliced backhand, in which you cut under the ball with the racket-head on impact. The chief problem of most children learning the backhand is to stop slicing every ball on the backhand side.

To play any of the three types of backhand, get your front foot forward so that you can get a good swing at the ball and don't have to make a punched or poking shot at it. Swing with freedom. Don't get the idea that you will get more control from a shortened back-swing.

The position of the feet—side-on to the net—is the whole secret of good, flowing backhand drives. The swing, the follow-through, and the transference of weight from the left to the right leg as you hit the ball all become automatic.

At the instant the racket strikes the ball, the arm holding it should be completely straight, with the arm, wrist, fingers and racket all in line. By getting that front foot across, you ensure that your body-weight supports this straight arm and that you don't just make the shot all arm-work.

The wrist dictates what type of backhand you will play by the angle at which it cocks the racket at the

53

Hoad's backhand in closeup: (1) He takes the racket back for an unrestricted swing, body side-on to net.

(2) His weight swings on to the front foot. His preliminaries in setting up the shot are unhurried, fluent.

(3) He watches the ball on to the strings, locking wrist on impact, and he makes contact in front of the body.

(4) He follows through after impact, putting all his weight behind the ball. Only now has he indicated direction of shot.

moment of impact. The top-spin backhand is the most effective because of the problems it gives your opponent in volleying. The top-spin makes the ball dip down into the court as it passes the net and means your rival has to hit up.

You hit a backhand sooner after the ball bounces than on the forehand. The earlier you hit it, the sharper will be your cross-court return. To hit it down the line, you delay your swing and strike the ball just behind the front hip.

The correct 'ready' position is vital when you hit a backhand return of service. By holding the racket straight out in front of the middle of your body, you can swing it quickly to forehand or backhand sides without losing any time.

Ken Rosewall probably has the best backhand in tennis today and he has hit some legendary shots with it, but I have played it so often since I was eleven years old that I can pick which way he will hit it from the type of ball it is, the way it approaches him and the way he lines up the shot. Ken has the ability to hit down the line on his backhand off a high or low ball. Off a ball of medium height, he is inclined to go cross-court on the backhand. Largely because of his lack of height, he cannot vary his

backhand range, however, and, well as he plays the shot, I don't have any fear of it. But a lot of other players never seem to get the knack of picking where Rosewall's backhand will go. Vic Seixas, for example, could never anticipate Rosewall's backhand, and I have seen Vic made almost helpless by it.

Tony Trabert, when he could get into position with that front foot across, probably had as good a backhand as you will ever see. His grip, footwork and timing were perfect, and he had a strong forearm to give extra power. But Trabert's weight reduced his mobility so much he often could not get into position to use these great backhand strengths.

I always enjoy playing backhands on the run because my strong forearm and wrist enable me to get weight into the stroke, however far I have to go to the left to reach the ball. Even if I can only just get to the ball, I can still impart top-spin to it and convert the shot into a winner.

It was a backhand on the run by Rosewall on our first visit to Wimbledon as seventeen-year-old kids, that really established us internationally for the first time. We had reached two sets all against Savitt and Mulloy. At five games all in the fifth set, the Americans led 40–30 on their service when Savitt lobbed over Rosewall's head for the first time in the match. We both scurried back from the net and we both shouted, 'Mine!' But Rosewall was better placed, and as we sprinted side-by-side, I veered away from the ball and he turned side-on, and from several yards behind the baseline, almost into the back-stopping, he hit a fabulous winner between Savitt and Mulloy as they closed into the net to volley away the return. That was the turning-point. We won the game and I served out the twelfth game for the match. My dad says he read the report of that match back in Australia five times.

Never run around your backhand. In top-class tennis there is just no time to move so that you can take every ball on the forehand, and you will only present your opponent with wide open spaces into which to hit his returns if you do so. Any ball that comes to your backhand side should be hit with a backhand.

I always thought Rex Hartwig had one of the best backhands I've encountered. 'Rekka' played Davis Cup with me in doubles, but never won the big tournaments his stroke play deserved, probably because of the way he would 'blow up' if the ball went somewhere he didn't intend. On high backhands he was dynamite, though, and in doubles he could whip that high ball across court

55

from up around his left ear like a rocket.

Study the great backhands of modern tennis, and look at the films of men like Donald Budge who played the shot so magnificently, and you will notice one common factor; they all get that front leg across quickly like soldiers going through a drill.

At no stage of his career has the great American, Pancho Gonzales, been regarded as a top-class backhand shotmaker. But he could control his backhand. It couldn't hurt you, but he could set up the ball for forehand winners with it. He had a tremendous forehand.

When I played Gonzales in a best-of-one-hundred matches as a professional, I quickly realized that with his hammer grip, fingers bunched on the handle, he could hit backhands only up the side line. I could hit the ball to his backhand and get across to the return in plenty of time to knock it off for a winner. When I was leading Gonzales by twenty-one matches to nine, he did an amazing thing which proved what a freak athlete he is: he changed his grip—a thing so fundamental to a tennis-player it was astounding Gonzales even tried it. But he spread his fingers along the handle in the approved Eastern grip, and overnight started to hit backhands across court. For the next three weeks, he hit crosscourt backhands, and before long the cross-court backhand became his best shot.

There are not many players like Gonzales around, thank Heaven, and we can't all expect to achieve his mastery so quickly, but if you forget the rubbish about the backhand being difficult you can make it a winning part of your tennis stroke-play.

Ken Rosewall's eyes remain fixed on the ball as he runs back to play a sliced backhand at Sydney's White City.

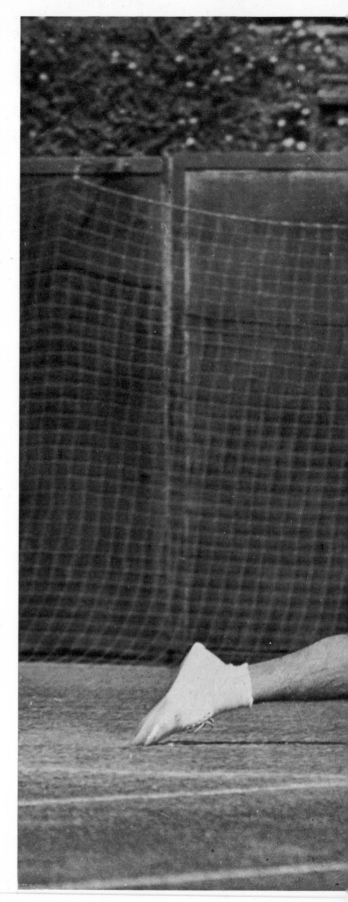

11 THE TROUBLE WITH GIRLS

Margaret Court

At seventeen, she was the youngest player and the first junior to win the Australian singles championship. Around the world, her brilliant performances since that win have confirmed that she is the finest woman tennis-player Australia has ever had and one of the best half dozen known to women's tennis. At her peak, her game has no weaknesses, she hits with the power of a man, and is probably as fast and as mobile as any woman has ever been, Suzanne Lenglen, Helen Wills-Moody and Maureen Connolly thrown in. Margaret was born on 16 July 1942, in the New South Wales border-town of Albury, where her father was the most popular man in town among local kids, for he was the district ice-cream maker. Margaret was a tomboy who kicked a football up and down her street with her two brothers and her elder sister, and bowled and batted at cricket. Just across from the Smith house were the courts of the Albury and Border Tennis Club, and here Margaret and her brothers staged guerrilla warfare with groundsman Wal Rutter, who finally gave up trying to chase her from the courts. Margaret moved to Melbourne and played her way through junior ranks to senior titles, and she followed a gymnasium routine that would make an international footballer shudder. At first, she worked in a room converted to a gymnasium in the Caulfield home of Percy Begbie, then in Frank Sedgman's gym under Stan Nicholes. She was coached by one of Victoria's top coaches, Keith Rodgers, then by Sedgman, and in 1962 on only her second world tour, missed the grand slam of the world's titles only through her first-round loss at Wimbledon. Few doubted that an unhappy feud with the L.T.A.A. helped cause this. In 1970 she made amends by becoming the first Australian woman and only the second woman (Maureen Connolly in 1953 was the other) to complete the grand slam. In 1971 she won her 10th Australian championship. Margaret Court now lives with her husband Barry in Claremont, Western Australia.

When I was a youngster in Albury, I had to be mobile to get a game. Usually three of us—my pals, Tom Spittle and Barry Hunt, and I—used to make sorties on to the courts where Wal Rutter was coach and curator.

Mr Rutter lived on the grounds, but we soon discovered that if we used one of the back courts a big hedge protected us from his view, provided the player at one end stayed at the net. The boys put me on the net at this end, and if I missed a ball and had to run back for it we were all thrown off. That must have been where I learned to volley!

Mobility is an absolute 'must' for any tennis-player, but this especially applies to women. They often have problems in getting to the ball. You just have to know how to run, which any man will tell you women players seldom can do.

A successful woman player has to have needle-sharp reflexes to cope with the unexpected shot she may be called on to play. And those same reflexes are needed to anticipate the direction and speed of the ball coming towards her. Generally, there is a little time to alter a stroke, but if you are sufficiently mobile you should be in position either to volley or play a forehand or backhand. Or, if the ball is high enough, you can change your stroke

Mobility is an absolute 'must' for any tennis player and particularly for women who often have problems in getting to the ball.

to a smash. And a smashed winner does more for your confidence than keeping the ball in play.

If your muscles are tight, you won't be able to get to the ball quickly enough. And if you are not fit, a lot of nervous tension builds up. I like to have a daily work-out in a gym and when I'm in Melbourne, my one and half hours a day with gym instructor Stan Nicholes, is an accepted part of my training. My routine includes weight-lifting—but no longer with the heavy weights—dumbells, wrist-curls, agility exercises, such as circuit-training, back-bending, 'swallows', double knee-jumps, jack-knives and legs over incline-board. I was on heavy weights when I first started. They were to build me up and make me stronger generally. Now I don't need them, I follow a set pattern five days a week.

I can also recommend squash for sharpening up reflexes and for keeping fit. Running is good, too, chiefly to build up stamina and to regulate breathing.

Individual coaching provides the ideal way of improving your stroke-production and mobility, but, because school classes and mass Saturday attendances make individual lessons almost impossible, tennis teachers have evolved effective ways of instructing groups.

The following schedules set out recommended class drills if mass instruction is unavoidable:

STARTING THEM OFF: Ask the class to face towards the net and stand with their feet apart, weight mainly on the toes, heels barely touching the court.

Tell them to relax the muscles and joints, and on the count of 'one', sway so that their weight is transferred to the right foot and the left leg is straightened. On the count of 'two' they should sway to the left so that the right leg is straightened. The effect of this exercise is to teach the pupils to loosen their hips and to show how weight transference is achieved. Practising this movement back and forth until they do it in a relaxed and fluent manner simulates the weight-transference used in backhand and forehand drives.

ROUTINE FOR FOREHAND: Organize the class with each pupil holding a racket in the Eastern grip recommended for the forehand and show the class how the whole forehand drive looks. Then break it up into stages for them and get them to copy each stage, numbering each one.

At the count of 'one', the class should turn side-on to the net, pivoting on the right foot and placing the left foot forward. On the count of 'two', the pupils take their left hands from the racket and swing the racket back, with the racket head roughly parallel to the ground, weight now on the right foot, knees slightly bent, shoulders turned more to the right. On the count of 'three', the racket swings forward to make contact with an imaginary ball slightly forward of the left hip, with the weight shifting to the left foot. The left knee is held firm at this point, and at the moment of impact, the racket is controlled by a locked wrist. The arm is straight so that all your reach is used. On the count of 'four', the class completes the follow-through, swinging the racket forward in the same plane as the earlier part of the stroke, with the wrist relaxing as the racket swings across the body and over the left shoulder. The body pivots around the left hip with the left leg braced. The shoulders and hips face the net at the end of the movement.

BACKHAND ROUTINE: Use the same drill as for the forehand. The first stage turns the class side-on to the net at the count of 'one'; the second stage produces the back-swing at the count of 'two'; the third stage, the swing through the ball on 'three'; the fourth stage, the follow-through on 'four', and the fifth stage, the return to the ready-position on 'five'.

GETTING TO THE BALL: Now that the class understands the parts of the forehand and backhand drives—as outlined more fully in other chapters of this book—the next step is to cultivate quick responses and to get them into position to play these strokes without stumbling or lack of co-ordination. Use a numbers system again, with the class moving sideways across the

The toe-tip balance of the great Brazilian Maria Bueno as she wins another Wimbledon title. She played some superb matches against Margaret Court.

Billie Jean King, one of America's greatest woman players.

As Margaret Court smashes she illustrates her agility. She has jumped well off the ground to hit the ball and even now, moments after contact, she is still airborne and well-balanced.

court to play a backhand on the count of 'one', and returning to play a forehand on the count of 'two'. They should move with a sort of skip-motion, and you should point out to them how the body-weight at the start of a stroke should be on the back foot and the body turned side-on into the ball as the swing begins. Then get them striding forward at angles to the right or left to pick up short balls. Other strokes like the service, volleys, half-volleys, smashes, and lobs can be practised in the same way. As a practice variation and as an aid to co-ordination, music can be introduced to the drills (waltz tempo or 2/4 time). You will notice that most of the exercises are designed in some way to make the pupil 'unbend' to improve his or her mobility.

If what I've said shows that I'm a crank on physical fitness, I make no apologies. You can't go on to the court with 'butterflies' and expect to win, but if you are fit, you shouldn't have 'butterflies'.

Skipping is a very good exercise for girls, particularly for developing speedy footwork. I don't do much skipping these days because I feel I've reached the stage where my footwork is just as I want it, but for anyone whose footwork is slow, skipping is ideal. Press-ups are valuable, too, because they develop the shoulder muscles; wrist-curls because they strengthen the all-important wrists.

All exercises are good, but some are better than others, and I suggest that a set pattern be followed. You can't beat being mobile. Take my word for it. Then read Ashley Cooper's chapter in this book on some of the exercises Australian Davis Cup teams use to get fit.

12 UNORTHODOXY—DOES IT PAY
Vivian McGrath

Quietly-spoken, retiring Vivian Bede McGrath came from a farming family in the New South Wales town of Mudgee. He was the first of the world's great two-handed players, a natural left-hander who toted what was probably the most devastating single shot tennis has known. This was the two-fisted backhand on the left side of his body. With it, boy wonder McGrath made an impact on tennis that will be talked about as long as the game lasts. He began his competitive tennis career while he was studying at Sydney High School, playing handicap matches for Eastern Suburbs Association. His rise was meteoric and at fourteen he was in the New South Wales Linton Cup team. At fifteen, he reached the last eight of the Australian Open singles beating former national champion Gar Moon. He beat the Japanese stars, Harada and Nunoi, in a match between Australia and Japan, and then beat the visiting American, Ellsworth Vines, reigning world champion, a feat which made him a world celebrity. He was just seventeen when he went overseas in 1933 with the Davis Cup team. In the next few years, he played an immense amount of tennis, competing in dozens of Cup matches, and tournaments in most world capitals. He won the 1937 Australian championship, but lost the title the next year to Donald Budge. McGrath, fleet-footed, wavy-haired, had had trouble with high arches, but it was a surfeit of tennis which put him out of the game at twenty-three. By 1939, he had had enough. Today he is a professional, teaching at private schools, mainly in New South Wales country centres, but his whipped, power-house two-hander remains an Australian sporting legend.

I saw a nine-year-old girl using a two-handed backhand out in western New South Wales recently, and I asked her why she kept two hands instead of one on the racket.

'Well,' she said, 'you can't hit a very dramatic back-hand with one hand—can you?'

I knew what she meant. There was that day in 1932 when I had used two hands to win the final point against Ellsworth Vines. I was sixteen and Vines was the world's champion, and here we were at match-point. I drove the ball straight down the line, everything behind it, timing just right. It was a terrific hit, and thirty years later the memory of it is strong. Often I have read that people said it was the most spectacular shot they had ever seen.

There were other shots I played with the two-hander, of course, that got the same result, but for me the one I hit that day against Ellsworth Vines to win 6–2, 2–6, 8–6, 7–5 in an Australian championship quarter-final was the shot that 'made' my tennis career.

Not many have used the two-hander in international tennis, but those who have often have done very well. I generally do not advise my pupils to use it. Of all the thousands of youngsters I've coached, I don't suppose I've urged more than half a dozen to use two hands, but

The 'Bounding Basque', Jean Borotra, in the beret that made him a famous figure in tennis. He kept playing at Wimbledon when well past fifty.

if the two-hander is a natural shot to a child, I believe it has strong advantages.

I know all about the shortcomings two-handed shots are supposed to have: the shortened reach, the inability to change sides quickly enough to volley well, and the so-called weakness of being taken out of court by a service that swings away from your double-handed side. But I am certain that if the two-hander is an instinctive stroke for you you should go on using it. I was lucky to have a bigger than normal reach, but for most people anticipation can make up for any lack of reach it causes, and it packs some tremendous advantages in arduous match-play because of the improved control it gives on ground-strokes.

The two-hander is perhaps the hardest shot of all for an opponent to anticipate because you can change its direction or even lob with it at the last instant. It has big advantages in controlling wrist-action for spin and direction. With a two-hander you can take the ball very early on the rise, and stand in close to receive service. It usually is hit close to the body, which increases the problem of detecting its direction. You can quickly master top-spin with it because the added control of two hands makes it easier to roll the racket over the ball. Holding the wrists back and restricting the follow-through, you can hit down the line with pinpoint accuracy. And you can just as easily snap the racket-head for a sharp cross-court shot.

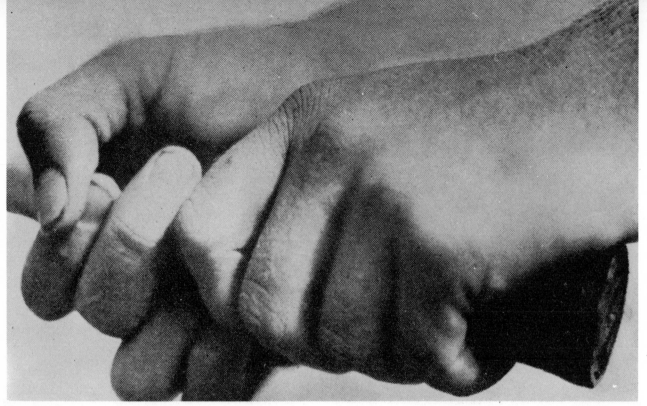

One of the most famous grips in tennis—John Bromwich's unorthodox two-handed grip. When he was playing well, Bromwich refused to let his rackets be cleaned for fear of upsetting their balance.

Most two-handers have very powerful left hands, and thus can play the forehand well on this side of their body. Very few use two hands on both sides of the body and I can recall only one or two players in a lifetime of tennis who used the two-hander for serving.

John Bromwich was ambidextrous. He served right-handed, hit his forehand with two hands, and his backhand with the left hand. He used a very loosely-strung racket on which the handle had been whittled to about the size of a shilling at the butt-end. His rackets used to be the despair of the sports-goods firm which made them because the friction of John's hands sliding up and down the handle made them very grimy. John did not like to have them cleaned when he was in good form for fear the cleaning might upset the balance. Bromwich had the greatest chip return of service in the history of tennis, an invaluable shot in doubles. He did not win a Wimbledon singles—he lost the 1948 final to Bob Falkenburg in five sets—but he won almost every other honour in the game and probably would have been more dominant with a good service.

Pancho Segura, of Ecuador, was one of the few top-liners to use two hands for both forehand and backhand. He placed the right hand above the left for both shots, holding the handle with an overlapping grip and using an extra length of leather wrapping on the handle. Like Bromwich, Segura lacked a really effective service.

Bromwich and Segura played the two-handed lob with great success, shaping to drive, and then throwing up lobs of beautiful length as they lured their opponents in to the net. Like them, I always found that I could deal severely with any balls that got up high on my two-handed side. Geoff. Brown, another Australian who did well with double-handed shots, used to swing himself almost off his feet putting away two-handed volleys.

The standard tactical approach against a two-handed player is to hit the ball low to him in the fore-court, exploiting his lack of reach and the slight slowness in changing sides in volleying. Often this lack of length in ground-strokes plays into the hands of the two-hander, who is able to exploit his superior ground-stroke control.

I did not link my hands with an overlapping grip, and I had no trouble, as some two-handers do, with slipping grips caused by sweat-stained handles. I volleyed and served right-handed, so I was not as vulnerable at the net as two-handers who persist with this style on the volley. I have always thought that the two-hander gave me an advantage in doubles, where it is vital to get the opposition's service back. On my first overseas tour in 1933, I reached the final of the British hardcourt doubles with Adrian Quist, losing the sixty-four-game final to Crawford and Turnbull. In Paris, Adrian and I were again finalists, beating Jean Borotra and Toto Brugnon, but losing the title to Fred Perry and Pat Hughes. Later, with Crawford, I won the Australian, Italian, German and French doubles.

From the first time I picked up a tennis racket to start learning the game, I used two hands for my backhand. I had never heard of or seen anyone who used two hands. Perhaps, like Segura, I started that way because the racket felt too heavy for me on that side, perhaps it was because I automatically felt I could get more control over the racket by using two hands. Whatever it was, the two-hander was completely natural to me. I played golf left-handed, was a left-handed batsmen at cricket, but I bowled right-arm and wrote right-handed.

At the time I arrived in top-line tennis, the only player with comparatively unorthodox strokes was Georgio de

Stefani, of Italy. De Stefani was ambidextrous and played all shots on his left-hand side with the left hand and all right-hand-side shots with the right hand. He served right-handed and had no backhand. This may have been why my two-handed style caused such international interest. I remember that in the beginning there was quite a lot of criticism of my style, which offended the purists, but I managed to silence this criticism by beating the Japanese, Harada and Nunoi, when I was fifteen, and then by defeating Vines, Allison, Van Ryn and Gledhill. At sixteen, I was the youngest Australian to gain Davis Cup selection, and the first double-handed player to compete in Davis Cup.

It is significant that John Bromwich and Geoff. Brown who followed me by reaching international class using two hands, had never seen me play when they put two hands on the racket. Bromwich was a seven-year-old who ball-boyed on his parents' court when he started in tennis, and he first put two hands on the racket because the first racket he swung was a full-sized model his parents used and was a little heavy for him. Brown, six years Bromwich's junior, had been using two hands for years before he saw Bromwich play.

Undoubtedly, my success encouraged Bromwich, and Bromwich's success encouraged Brown at a time when their two-handed styles were being criticized; we all learnt the style naturally, but played our two-handers differently. That is why I believe there always will be two-handed players, although they may never dominate the game as appeared possible when I beat 'Brom' 6–3, 1–6, 6–0, 2–6, 6–1 in a two-handers final of the 1937 Australian singles.

The Italian, Beppi Merlo, beat many of the world's best players using a two-handed grip. He used to reach across his body to play a two-handed shot on the left-hand side, his right hand reaching further down the handle than the left. Bob Howe won one Wimbledon Mixed Doubles title with a two-handed game. Talk to any one of them, and you will find they adopted their two-handed styles instinctively.

If the double-handed shots come naturally to you and you are confident you can build a good all-round stroke repertoire in which you can properly exploit the two-handed shot's advantages, do not let the theorists discourage you. Considering how few have tried two-handed shots, the two-handed style has a very good record. At its best it can be devastating.

Vivian McGrath, the world's first top-ranking two-handed player. He did not link his hands with an overlapping grip as most two-handers do, but had no trouble with sliding fingers.

13 VOLLEYS NEED PUNCH
Jack Pollard

Nothing has played a bigger part in speeding up tennis than the wide improvement in volleying standards. With the swing to net-rushing tactics among the world's major title-winners, the volley has become more important than good ground-strokes. Today, titles can be won with a first-rate service and a reliable, authoritative volley. It is possible to play reasonable singles without being able to volley well, but it is not possible to reach the highest class as a singles player without it. The shot is absolutely essential if you are to play doubles of any standard at all. The modern brand of tennis in which speed in moving to the net is combined with fast reflexes, agility and anticipation rests heavily on the player's volleying skill. Indeed volleying—the art of hitting the ball before it has bounced—has been a hallmark of all the Australian Davis Cup teams that in the last decade have built such a formidable record. Volleying skill is a trade-mark of Harry Hopman's coaching, too. It is the shot which converted Australian tennis from base-line stuff to the mixture of speed, power and sparkling net-attack it is today.

Most of the accomplished volleyers in tennis—players like Ken Rosewall, Lew Hoad, Margaret Court, Frank Sedgman and Rod Laver—hit the ball with slight spin, the racket moving under the ball at the moment of contact. This gives control which is not possible when you hit the ball flat. The great players seldom hit a volley completely flat unless the ball comes to them well above the net, so that they can sweep it away with the same swing they use on drives.

Many players in amateur tournaments seek to cover their ground-stroke weaknesses by going to the net on every ball, whatever the length of the shot on which they go in. This has little prospect of success against first-class opposition, but it applies a psychological pressure inexperienced competitors can seldom throw off. Perhaps this is so because beginners often shy clear of going to the net, and treat the fore-court as a danger area. They seem to feel they will be struck in the face if they venture away from the base-line, and you will frequently see novices duck or cover their faces if they are lured near to the net. The danger is non-existent, of course, if they keep their eyes on the ball and have the racket ready to protect themselves.

Volleying techniques vary, but they all have certain virtues in common. These virtues are fast reflexes, quick positioning of the feet and racket, a firm grip at the moment of contact and keeping the eyes on the ball.

Neale Fraser playing a backhand volley with both feet off the ground. He was a player of rare courage who never gave up.

There used to be an adage in tennis that a good volley was valueless if poor ground-strokes prevented you from getting into position to use it. But many of today's tournament players are giving this idea a shake, covering up their lack of ground-strokes with agility, a big service and anticipation which enables them to put away shots that seem to have passed them. The art of making good passing shots has, in fact, slumped as more and more players appeared with reasonably good volleys.

The volley is a short, clipped, downward blow, played with the body sideways on to the net, a half-stroke played with punch. The stars are unanimous that the secret is to get down to it—to bend your knees. There is no need for back-swing because, if you get into position to volley, your opponent has usually been forced to hurry his stroke and the ball comes to you at increased speed, which compensates for the normal back-swing.

Budge Patty, the nomad American who won Wimbledon and a hatful of titles around the European circuit, was probably one of the most reliable volleyers of his period. But he used almost no back-swing, pushing into the ball after contact with a characteristic wrist-action similar to that used by good squash-players.

Australian Davis Cup players since 1950 have invariably been first-rate exponents of the volley. Harry Hopman, who coached every Australian team until 1969 often stood one player at the net while two, three or even four others hit sizzling ground-strokes to him from the back of the opposite court. It's arduous work, likely to reduce all but the very fit to a grease-spot, but it very quickly improves volleying skills.

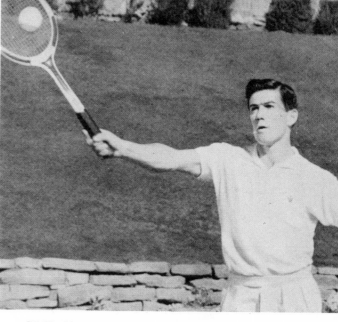

KEN ROSEWALL ON HOW TO VOLLEY

(1) FOREHAND VOLLEY

Eyes concentrated on the ball, he takes a very short backswing, using same grip as for driving. The head of the racket must be above wrist, ball out in front. At the moment of impact, the wrist is firmly locked. The racket strings punch the ball. Contact has been made in the very middle of the racket strings.

(2) BACKHAND VOLLEY

The weight of the body transfers to the right foot as the ball is hit. The grip is the same as for the backhand drive, the action short, punched, body side-on to the net. The ball is hit in front of the body. In this shot Rosewall has not got his right leg as far across as he should. But his concentration is admirably sustained.

GRIP AND STANCE: These are the same as those used for the backhand and forehand drives, although some players hold the racket further up the handle, shortening their reach a little to get added control. Callisthenics and continual squeezing of a squash ball or the steel springs sold in many sports shops for wrist-strengthening can eliminate the need for this 'choking' on the handle.

TIMING: To ensure you control the volley, you should make contact with the ball further in advance of your body than on the backhand or forehand drives. The head of the racket must always be above the wrist, which is locked on impact. You are so much closer to the opposition than in playing ground-strokes that there is no

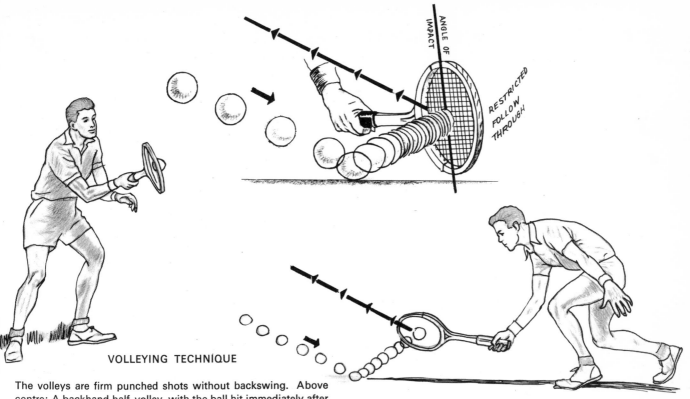

VOLLEYING TECHNIQUE

The volleys are firm punched shots without backswing. Above centre: A backhand half-volley, with the ball hit immediately after bouncing. Above left: A forehand volley at the moment of impact, the player side-on to the net, wrist locked. Above right: A forehand half-volley, with the drawing slightly exaggerated to show puzzled youngsters how the ball is stroked immediately after it bounces. Pace already on ball is exploited.

Jack Kramer (U.S.A.), volleying against Australia's **Geoff Brown** at Wimbledon. Note the firm grip he employs.

time for back-swing. Don't let the ball come to you—go to meet it.

FIRST VOLLEYS: Some top-liners never attempt to hit their first volleys beyond their opponent's service-line. They reason that getting in close to the net puts pressure on their opponent, who is far more likely to give them an easier shot to put away on the second volley. Thus, it's a good rule not to try for a winner on your first volley unless you spot a clear gap into which you can hit the ball.

FOOTWORK: Quickly getting your feet into position is one of the keys to this shot, whether the ball arrives on the backhand or the forehand. The feet will move more quickly if you are on your toes instead of slumped on the heels. For the forehand volley, the left foot goes across in front of your body, as it does for the forehand drive, until you are side-on to the net and facing the side-lines. For the backhand volley, the right foot moves promptly forward and across the body to about the same position as for the backhand drive. Turning of the body for either forehand or backhand volleys is brought about by this step with left or right foot.

Charlie Hollis, the Queensland coach who started Rod Laver and Mal Anderson on the trails that led them to world fame, has repeatedly told me that good volleying starts with the 'ready' position. Hollis teaches his pupils to hold the racket well in front of the centre of the body, gripped firmly by the non-striking hand at the throat of the racket and loosely by the fingers of the striking hand. The non-striking hand firmly pushes the racket to left or right as the player anticipates a backhand or forehand shot and he selects his grip on the handle.

CONTROLLING DIRECTION: On the forehand volley, if you wish to punch the ball to the right, get your front foot further across and play the shot a fraction late. To angle the ball to the left, hit the ball slightly earlier than for volleys straight down the court. On the backhand

Fred Perry, a great exponent of the volley, shows the quick reflexes essential near the net.

Although he had to bend low to make this volley, Rod Laver has retained complete control of the racket.

side, you volley to the right by striking the ball with your left foot further across and a little further in front of you. To volley to the left on the backhand side, you make contact slightly earlier, and with the back foot slightly further back.

To reach the highest standards of the game, it is important to develop a backhand volley as sound as your forehand volley. If you don't volley well on both sides, opponents will quickly learn to direct their passing shots to your inferior side, even luring you to the net to do this.

Remember in all types of volleys that the reason for the cross-step—in which the foot opposite the side you will hit the stroke moves forward—is that you can cover twice as much ground as with a side-step. The cross-step adds sharpness to your volley and helps produce the crisp timing required.

THE DROP VOLLEY: This is a shot for advanced pupils, in which the wrist is loosened slightly on impact instead of being held firmly locked. The effect is to impart chop that gives the ball backspin. It is used mainly when you have to play the ball close to the net from below the top of the net. It demands rare touch, and if you can, hit down on the ball instead of trying the drop-volley.

MISSED VOLLEYS: Before you blame your opponent's speed or spin for those flubbed volleys, examine your execution of them. Are you standing too near the net? Are you a step late in getting in to volley? Are you committing the common mistake of taking your eye from the ball to watch the spot where the ball is to go?

If you are a natural net-player, do not try to stay back when you find yourself passed a few times. The percentages are in your favour and against the ground-stroke player who has to keep making accurate passing shots. It would be fatal to play an unnatural game from the base-line. Constant pressure is the secret.

14 PERCENTAGE TENNIS—WHAT IT MEANS

Roy Emerson

Roy Stanley Emerson, born 3 November 1936, is a farmer's son from the Queensland peanut centre, Kingaroy. His family built a court on their farm, and at ten, Roy started the climb to tennis stardom which has taken him to Wimbledon championships, Davis Cup selection, the singles championships of Australia, France and the U.S., and to important doubles crowns (Wimbledon twice, French six times, Australian twice and Italian three times). Emerson was an outstanding schoolboy athlete before he decided to concentrate on tennis, and he took a legacy of great speed into tennis. He won all the Queensland age-group titles—under-twelve, under-fourteen, under-sixteen—and then cleaned up junior titles of Australia. He was in Queensland's Linton Cup team at seventeen in 1952, the year he made his first overseas tour under Harry Hopman. He missed a world tour in 1953, went round again in 1954, 1955, 1956 and 1957, and in 1958 stayed home to marry Mavis Joy Auld, who was well known in Queensland women's tennis. They bought a house in Brisbane in 1962, and shortly afterwards, Emerson, dickering with thoughts of becoming a professional, took a public relations job with the Phillip Morris Tobacco Company which ensured he would remain an amateur at least until 1965. When Laver left amateur tennis to become a professional after the 1962 Challenge Round, critics said this left Emerson the world's No 1 amateur. Emerson vindicated this judgment by winning five straight Australian singles between 1963 and 1967, when he turned professional. He remains one of the world's top players, with many big professional wins behind him, earning $100,000-a-year.

Matches are won, not by players who hit spectacular winners, but by players who always get the ball back. This has been shown again and again since the early days of tennis. The essence of making the percentages work for you by getting every ball back is never to try to make an impossible shot. Always keep your shotmaking within your capabilities. Don't try to raise the chalk by hitting the lines when a ball a yard inside the lines will win the point.

I often have been called a percentage player, largely, I think, because I have a good pair of legs, and can get round the court and make some good retrieves. This enables me to get to balls which might otherwise be winners. Rod Laver and America's 'Chuck' McKinley have good legs and their fine results show how important it is to chase every ball.

The trick is to make your opponent earn every point: if you keep getting them back, you increase the pressure on him to put it away, and this forces him into errors.

It's important that when you are badly out of position you should throw up a high lob which will give you time to get back to the centre of the court. Get that lob up high, and you are still well in the fight for a point. This does not mean that percentage or defensive tennis hangs on the use of the lob—there is more to it than just putting the ball in the air—but it has a psychological effect on your opponent if he knows you are a player who won't let the ball go by and that you will be getting many of his

Rod Laver, with one of his US singles trophies. He has been one of the classic exponents of percentage tennis, always giving the impression that he had something in reserve and sharply reducing his number of errors.

best shots back. It is likely to make him try for extra power and hit closer to the lines, and thus increase his errors.

I play every point as a big point, especially the very first point in a match. This is an important point to win—take the next and you are already well in front.

It is heartbreaking to play an excellent retriever, particularly on hardcourt or clay, where the slower surface makes it tougher than on grass to put the ball away. But it's worse still if you know your retriever opponent is a master of the defensive lob, for you know that you are going to have to concentrate particularly hard. You can't hit him off the court. You are going to be out there a long time. You can take a set 6–0 and take an hour to do it. In Europe, where most of the successful players have good legs, it is not unusual for a three-setter to take three hours. I played four games once in Hamburg against a retriever while the South Africans, Gordon Forbes and Abe Segal, played an entire doubles match. The first set of one match there took four hours, and they counted up that the ball passed over the net three hundred times for one point!

In the first or second rounds of Australian tournaments, you generally can count on matches lasting an hour, but in Europe you can be out there two and a half hours in the first match of a tournament. There used to be a joke among the top players of the amateur circuit that if you played the Italian, Fausto Gardini, on a hot day you would end up with a sore mouth. Most players hit smashes with their mouths open. They reckoned that the two hundred odd smashes you had to play against Gardini with the sun on the roof of your mouth caused the soreness.

Under the watchful eye of one time Australian tennis boss, 'Big Bill' Edwards, of Queensland, American Tony Trabert approaches a buffet table. Trabert overcame a lack of mobility by reducing his percentage of mistakes.

Gardini, Herbie Flam, Neale Fraser, Ted Schroeder, Vic Seixas, Pancho Segura and Ken Rosewall were about the best retrievers I've seen. Fraser didn't have good ground-shots, but he got to the top because he ran for everything and because he could play high defensive lobs. Fraser won a Davis Cup challenge round point that gave Australia the Cup back in 1961 by putting a lob over six-foot four-inch Barry MacKay's head. Art ('Tappy') Larsen won the final of the American singles by taking the final point with a lob which lifted chalk from the base-line. Playing Gardini, you would move in to the net behind a good approach shot and find yourself following a high lob back to the base-line.

All of these good 'percentage' players were masters of the high lob. For example, Rosewall has a great attacking lob which gets the volleyer off balance and has the volleyer diving to scramble the ball back. His lob is just high and quick enough to get over the top of a player at the net, but it seems to die once it bounces. The top-spin makes the ball 'sit' and run away from his opponent instead of bouncing high. In the art of hitting up from under the ball and imparting top-spin, Rosewall and Rod Laver are the best I have seen. Running wide to a ball deep on his forehand side, Laver can play a magnificent top-spin lob, rolling the racket over the ball at the moment of impact. He does it with the same swing as for a forehand down the line and it is very hard to anticipate. It is almost always a winner, because it is such a complete surprise and because it takes a very fast player to get back behind it before the top-spin makes it die. A warning here—don't try for top-spin lobs on the backhand side, only on forehands.

Another feature of good percentage tennis is that the players who exploit it best usually have a very good block-shot with which to return a fast service. Serving to Rosewall, you always feel that you just don't have anywhere to hit the ball. Wherever you place your service you seem to get it back low and at your feet. This goes through your mind all the time you are serving to him, and the thought works on you and your serving falls away. This is one of the big advantages he has—the trick of making his rivals feel that it's futile serving to him. A lot of players can play the block-shot well off powerful services, but they spoil the effect of this by failing to get in to the net right behind it.

Here are some guiding principles of 'percentage' tennis:
- The time to throw up a defensive lob is when you are in no position to play anything else.
- Throw your lobs up high from defensive positions to give your opponent's nerves a chance to work for you and to give you (and your partner) time to get back into position.
- Remember that a smash takes more out of a man than any other shot. Every smash hurts in the fifth set: that's why the lob is so effective.
- In doubles, when the opposition sends up a lob over your man at the net, the best reply always is to put up another high defensive lob. The odds are against you if you try to drive across court from that position. Your opponents will have moved in to the net behind their lob, so they will have to let your return lob bounce.
- Give it a go, however hopeless your position, however much you are unbalanced. Don't give up. You don't really get into the match until you start chasing everything. I have seen players win points in Davis Cup ties by hitting the ball behind their backs.
- Remember that the running involved in 'percentage' tennis will get you into better physical shape and thus increase the benefit you get from the game. And there is no satisfaction quite like returning an apparently certain winner.

Anyone can play five sets at their own speed, but to play them running all the time is tough. Laver brings off one of his best shots—a running forehand—off balls which he is absolutely flat out to reach at all. If he didn't run he would never be in a position to make it.

There is one mistake to guard against in playing percentage tennis: that is, that in your eagerness to get every ball back, you neglect to stroke the ball, and start prodding and patting it. You should always hit the ball fluently and make your strokes as you have been taught to do—but don't ask too much of your stroke-repertoire. Keep control of it. Concentrate, concentrate, never forgetting that tennis matches are not won on winners: they are lost on errors.

At Sydney's White City, American Dennis Ralston hits a smash.

15 TOURNAMENT TENNIS

John Newcombe

John Newcombe, a nephew of Australian Test cricketer Warren Bardsley, was born in Sydney on 23 May 1944. He was educated at Sydney Grammar School, where he developed a taste for books and an ability to think which was no handicap at all later on. Helped by a big service and a willingness to work hard he developed quickly as a tennis player and in 1961 won the first of his three successive Australian junior titles. In 1963, he made his Davis Cup debut at the age of 19 in Adelaide, performing with great credit against the experienced Americans Dennis Ralston and Chuck McKinley. Ralston had to go to a 7–5 fifth set to win, and almost every game of the four sets McKinley took to beat Newcombe was prolonged and tense. An outstanding doubles player, Newcombe won the Wimbledon doubles in 1965 with Tony Roche, retained it in 1966 with Ken Fletcher, and won it again with Roche in 1968–69–70. He was Wimbledon and U.S. singles champion in 1967, and after the Challenge Round that year in Brisbane turned professional for a guarantee of $126,000 for three years. He also married in 1967. His wife, Angelika Pfannenburg, of Hamburg, became a naturalised Australian in 1968. They have a three-year-old son, Clint. Newcombe's fondness for politics, his wide popularity and high I.Q. made him an ideal President of the International Tennis Players' Association when it was formed in 1969. Immediately, he became a keen advocate of a more professional approach to tennis promotion and an ardent supporter of admitting professionals to the Davis Cup. In between arduous tours he laid the foundation for a big future in business, putting a lot of money into a tennis ranch in San Antonio, Texas, and a racket club in Dallas. In 1970, Newcombe and Ken Rosewall played the 10th all-Australian Wimbledon singles final since the war, Newcombe winning his second title 5–7, 6–3, 6–2, 3–6, 6–1. And in 1971 John Newcombe defeated American Stan Smith to take out his third men's single championship. Newcombe has proved himself a great professional, of cool efficiency.

In tennis, it is not enough to learn to execute every shot brilliantly on all types of surfaces and to master all the tactical variations of the game. The essential thing is to be able to use these skills under the stress of competitive play. For it is one of the piquant fascinations of tennis that a game which worked impressively at practice so frequently falls apart when exposed to the tensions of tournament play.

Social tennis can be fun, but tournaments are the life blood of the game. This is why every youngster should start to play in tournaments as soon as the fundamentals have been learned. Even at the lowest levels, tournament tennis is more rewarding for players with ambition than a casual match. Many of the world's greatest players began in low age group tournaments. Lew Hoad played in the Manly Seaside tournament at ten. Ken Rosewall was the talk of Illawarra grade tennis at nine.

There is, however, a right and a wrong way to approach a tennis tournament, and it is wise to give thought to this before the first service is struck. You should be fit enough to play extended rallies without running out of puff. You should be properly attired and equipped along the lines recommended by Ken McGregor in his chapter of this book. Most Australian youngsters do enough running at school or at play after it to develop sound legs and provided they do not over-eat or eat all the wrong things should be fit for tennis without special gymnasium work-

outs. But as they reach the higher standards of tennis they will learn the benefits of two or three long runs each week.

At Sydney's White City in 1970 I learned a lesson about equipment which I should have absorbed ten years before. I changed into spiked shoes after 16 games in the rain against Dennis Ralston and found the spikes were half a size too small. The court was so wet I had to wear spikes so for the next four hours I played with bruised toes. I had neglected the cardinal rule of trying out my equipment.

Another golden rule for successful tournament play is to arrive at the courts early enough to have a hit before your match begins. I don't mean just the hit up on the match court with your opponent, but a good solid 20-minute session out on a back court where you can get your ground shots, volleys and service grooved.

Often in pro. tennis we run into trouble because we do not have sufficient time to practise on a strange surface before our matches. At Detroit in 1970 I lost a match in straight sets to Pancho Gonzales which was worth $10,000 to the winner. We played on a surface known as Uni-turf, which I had not been on for seven months. We used American balls which are much lighter and flightier than the Australian balls I had used just before I flew into Detroit. I am sure I would have pushed Pancho all the way had I had time to condition myself to these things.

Even courts of the same material can vary in pace and bounce from one district to another. The ball may bounce high in the Sydney suburb of Balmain but keep low at

John Newcombe, a cool, efficient player, has a big service and a willingness to work hard.

Tony Roche, one of the world's most successful tournament players, makes a high return.

Centre court at Wimbledon.

Pratten Park only a few miles away. The lesson is obvious—try to get some practice on the courts on which your tournament matches are to be played. If you cannot manage this at least try to get an extended hit-up on the strange court. Talk to the players at Country Week in Sydney and they will all emphasise how much better they handle the grass courts of White City at the end of the week than they did at the start of the week when they were fresh from clay courts.

All of us suffer from nervousness at times during a match. Even the game's greatest players can recall moments when tension transformed their tennis to a shambles. One year in the Challenge Round at Brisbane Australia's Ashley Cooper became so edgy he could barely toss the ball up to serve—several times, in fact, the ball stayed in his palm when he made the toss-up action. Rod Laver got to within three points of his first grand slam in 1962 against Roy Emerson at Forest Hills when his whole game seemed to fall apart.

'My fingers couldn't seem to find any of my usual grips on the racket handle, and my mouth was suddenly very parched,' Laver said. 'The racket felt as if it was being tugged away from me by an invisible hand and my leg muscles were on fire. I was out of control.'

Laver got himself under control again, however, and won the match to complete the first grand slam since Donald Budge did it back in 1938. He did not let those few moments of torment beat him. It is something we all have to learn to do, particularly when we first begin in tournaments. Fitness helps and so perhaps will a few deep breaths. But you have to recognise in advance that you are going to be confronted occasionally by extreme nervous tension and tell yourself that you will whip it.

The other important aspect of retaining poise during your tournament matches is to make up your mind that bad decisions or lucky net-cords that go your opponent's way are not going to upset you. It has often been said that the pros. are much more tolerant of doubtful line decisions than leading amateurs. This is because they realise mistakes can occur but are determined they will not spoil their concentration on the points which follow.

In my amateur days I played in tournaments in which players sometimes argued with umpires or tried to 'pull a fast one' on the umpire or their opponent. This is very rare in pro. tennis because all the pros. realise this kind of behaviour will not benefit them during the match concerned or on the rest of the professional circuit.

In the 1970 Wimbledon final against Ken Rosewall I could have allowed the partisan barracking for Rosewall to upset me had I not trained myself for years to overcome tournament distractions. I felt rankled that Ken's winners were cheered but mine were greeted by near silence. I felt like shouting out to the crowd, 'Heck I want to win this darn title, too, you know.' It was pretty bad when Ken reached two sets all, but I kept my cool well enough to win the fifth set fairly easily.

There is only one Wimbledon, of course. Of all the tournaments open to a tennis player it stands apart, with standard of organisation to equal its unique prestige. I only wish Australia had a tournament which remotely

The stress of playing tennis before an audience like this, requires years of preparation. Nearly 18,000 people atttended each day's play in this 1958 Challenge Round at Brisbane in which the USA defeated Australia.

approached Wimbledon's promotional efficiency.

One of the ironies of tennis in recent times has been that Australia, the country which produces the world's finest players, also has become notorious as the nation which runs the worst tournaments. All the Australians on the pro. circuit wish this was not so, but the facts have to be faced. Running big tournaments is a job for professional promoters and Australia for too long allowed her tournaments to be run by part-time amateurs. It will be very difficult now that she has squandered public support for even the most skilful promoters to get big crowds back, but all of us hope that the efforts of L.T.A.A. President Wayne Reid and sponsors like Dunlop will do the trick.

Often in the past decade, when so many tennis traditions were changed, the failure of Australian officials to meet and talk with players during their tournaments cost Australia very dearly. Australian administrators slavishly adhered to rules other nations broke with impunity. Strangely enough, in the big years of the amateur circuits in Europe and South America, Australians collected more appearance money than players from other nations, all of it overseas.

The international tournament scene has changed a lot since then, with more and more big centres competing for professional instead of amateur tournaments and almost all the big names taking their money openly. The great pity of all this is that open tennis was not introduced until 1968 when it should have been sanctioned back in 1961. Equally mystifying is the failure of the International Lawn Tennis Federation to give professionals a voice in their mediations after the I.L.T.F. agreed to open tournaments and thus created a large permanent group of professionals.

The tournament life of top players is about ten years and in that short period of prime life the pro. tennis player must ensure his entire future. This is why we formed the International Tennis Player's Association in 1969—we wanted to ensure that tournaments were properly run. The playing conditions at tournaments have been at the top of our thinking ever since. Dressing-room facilities, court surfaces, securing experienced umpires, linesmen and ball boys are some of these. The public who pay to watch us and have been somewhat neglected at past tournaments are also our concern, and we have worked to get superior spectator comfort.

It is no accident that the best tennis crowds go to the best-appointed tennis arenas. Wimbledon, Wembley, Madison Square Garden, The Spectrum in Philadelphia and stadiums like them which offer customers seats close to the matches and have plenty of dining and drinking (soft or hard) facilities are repeatedly packed for tournament play. There is a big future, too, for the tournament which combines with social functions. A couple of years ago in Dallas eight women players raised $25,000 in three days on courts which seated only 300 people. People gladly paid $1,000 for the three days for boxes with six seats in them. Three day single seats had ample takers at $50 each. Success stemmed from the fact that there were big parties on Friday and Saturday night for all the people who bought seats to the tennis. That's the kind of new approach to tournament psychology Australian tennis badly needs.

16 KILL THAT SMASH!

Billy Sidwell

Oswald William Thomas Sidwell was born in the New South Wales city of Goulburn in 1920, son of ardent lawn bowlers. His father played tennis well enough to compete against Crawford and McGrath, and Bill inherited his dad's interest in the game. Bill won the Australian boys' doubles in 1938 with Pails and the singles in 1939. He played tennis for the R.A.A.F. in the war, Rugby League as a bruising hooker, soccer as a centre-half. Sidwell, who had had a job waiting for him with Slazengers when he left school, played singles and doubles for the 1948–49 Australian Davis Cup teams. He was runner-up in the 1947 Wimbledon doubles with Tony Mottram, beating Pails and Bromwich in the semi-finals, losing to Falkenburg and Kramer in the final. He won the Victorian singles in 1948–49 and the 1947 Australian hardcourt doubles with Quist. In the 1948 Davis Cup inter-zone final, he had a great three-sets-to-one win over Drobny. The next year, he won the U.S. doubles with Bromwich, and in 1950, he won the German doubles with Quist, and was runner-up again in the Wimbledon doubles with Brown, losing to Bromwich and Quist in an exciting final. Sidwell always played in a peaked cap which he said prevented him squinting and he was noted for fiery overheads, often soaring feet off the ground to hammer away a smash. He is now a senior executive of Slazengers, lives at Bondi, Sydney, has three handsome children, plays very keen golf off a handicap of one.

Anyone who can serve can smash. Basically, the forehand smash and the serve are identical strokes. This means that the smash, though spectacular, satisfying and a surefire points-winner, is one of the easiest strokes in tennis. Yet a remarkably small percentage of social players use the shot with real competence. For too many of them, the smash is a hopeful hit-or-miss whack at the ball. As often as not, this kind of stroke—if you could call it a stroke—puts the ball into the net or out of court. So, many players who try the smash eventually become afraid of it.

This needless lack of confidence is born of ignorance of the simple techniques of the smash—the properly executed smash is a controlled adaptation of perfectly natural movement.

The player who learns to smash improves his game enormously. The smash not only wins him many points: it gives him added confidence that lifts his all-round game; it enables him to take the initiative when under pressure in a rally; it worries his opponent into caution not to set up anything he might smash, and this, of course, will grievously affect the other fellow's game.

Apart from all this, the smash essentially is a basic part of any properly equipped player's game. But it is not enough that he should master only the forehand smash, the game's 'big' shot. He must also learn the arts of playing all other shots above the chest.

In learning to master the techniques, you will duff many of your attempts to smash. Don't be discouraged. The main thing is that you should go about it in the right way. As practice makes you more proficient in all phases of overhead play, you will find more enjoyment in your tennis and will move into more skilled company.

The average player could reach many more balls with his feet off the ground than he would believe. This is because the action of going up is largely instinctive. Children who are pleased about something jump to express their joy. And let me remind you that when you

Neale Fraser about to smash a return.

want to indicate something you point unerringly to it, without necessarily looking at the object. Your sense of location guides your arm or your finger.

Leaving the ground to smash a tennis ball is a controlled movement that adapts the natural human impulse to jump in the air and the common facility for pointing things out.

Your natural sense of timing and location will tell you when to take off and at what point to make contact with the ball. Whether you do this well or indifferently will depend, to a degree, on how much practice you give to it and how much confidence you have in yourself. Don't be a timid smasher. Go up boldly and really try to bury that ball!

Even some great players have been reluctant to leave the ground to smash—until they found out how easy it was. One of these was Englishman Tony Mottram, with whom I reached a Wimbledon doubles final (Americans Kramer and Falkenburg beat us for the title). Tony was a good smasher with his feet on the ground, but he would not jump. He was a pretty big man and he convinced himself he could reach pretty well anything without getting into the air. But I believe he lacked confidence in his ability to control mid-air smashes until his coach, Dan Maskell, persuaded him to try. Then he became a most competent off-the-ground smasher. John Bromwich, for a long time, would not jump because he thought he would lose control—until he tried it. Then he became as polished at this as at all other phases of the game.

Mention of the ambidextrous Bromwich reminds me to point out that in this chapter I address myself to right-handers, since they outnumber the southpaws. Left-handers should read everything I say in reverse.

For the smash, the grip may be the Continental or Eastern backhand, with the fingers spread well apart. Choose whichever is the more comfortable. I recommend the Eastern backhand, but only if it is comfortable. There was one great player who used the Eastern forehand grip on overheads—Ted Schroeder—who used it also in his

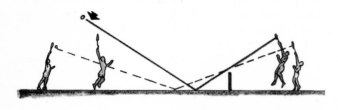

Never practise the smash until you are warmed up. Overheads are big, heavy strokes hit hard, with stomach, back and shoulder muscles behind them. The smash is the easiest points-winner of all for a champion, the most difficult in tennis for beginners. Stars thrive on them, bouncing them over the fence, angling them away. The novice overhits or underhits them, backing away or falling into the ball. The reason is that in an average match players hit far fewer smashes than other shots. Thus a novice should rehearse overheads more than other strokes to compensate for lack of match practice with it. The ball should be hit a foot in front of the head. Timing depends on a rhythmical swing. Only difference between a serve and a smash is the angle of the racket face on impact. Confidence in your smash permeates your game, and completely demoralises your rival.

On pages 82 and 83 Lew Hoad shows how to smash:

(1) Catlike in movement, he assesses the shot. (2) He starts to position himself, eyes intent on the ball. (3) He takes racket back, eyes still on ball. (4) He throws up his free arm as a sighter to the ball, weight on the back foot. (5) He leaves the ground, floating up to get under the ball as if by instinct. (6) He watches the ball right on to the swung rackethead. (7) Instinctively he starts to angle the ball by turning the wrist on impact. (8) He follows through across and down the body.

service. This grip does not suit most players, however, because it almost prevents the essential wrist-snap.

FOREHAND SMASH: This is played with the left shoulder facing the net. The racket-head is moved from rest in the left hand to a position parallel with the ground. The right hand drops it down and back in an arc to the rear, as for the serve. The wing, up and forward, is identical with the service movement, as is the follow-through. But the player must concentrate on this essential difference: he is not propelling the ball in the air with the free hand before striking it and he must judge the position in which the ball to be smashed will come to him. A sense of timing will tell him at what height to make contact with the ball.

The ball is struck with the full face of the racket, but with the head slightly closed. This is because the ball must be hit down at an angle to keep it in court but not so sharply that it will go into the net. The wrist-snap partly closes the racket-head and gives the ball maximum speed on contact.

Full follow-through is essential. Otherwise the ball will merely pop off the racket and the would-be smasher will have no control of the direction it will take.

LEAVING THE GROUND: If the player is agile enough, he should leave the ground, where this is practicable, to meet the ball at the greatest height he can reach. This gives him many advantages. He can bring down the ball at a sharper angle than if he remained on the ground, thereby giving his smash greater depth and bounce. By going up, he ensures he can hit down on the ball, imparting more speed and gaining greater control of placement. And—though this seems anomalous—he has more time to get into position to smash while in the air than he would have on the ground: he is able to bend back, if necessary, to adjust his hitting position with no loss of balance. And he is in a better position in the air than on the ground to judge the moment for the most effective contact.

THE JUMP: The proper technique for leaping to smash simulates the movements of a panther springing on its prey. As you watch the ball make its high arc from your opponent's racket, you are back on your haunches anticipating the line of fall and judging the moment to spring. You take off from the right foot, which has been drawn back from the left and has taken most of the body weight. Up you go, with the left leg lifting sharply as the knee bends in a natural balancing movement, then straightening so that you come down first on the left foot. Get plenty of spring into your take-off, so that you get well up into the air, thereby giving yourself more time to get into position for the 'kill'.

JUDGING THE LOB: Most players lob in a pattern. Some favour the high lob, some a lower trajectory; some impart over-spin, some back-spin, some play the shot with a flat racket that imparts no spin at all.

If you are familiar with your opponent's style in this department, you will be in a good position to anticipate his shot, and therefore should have plenty of time to get into position to smash it. If you do not know his game, try to size up his lobbing style as quickly as possible.

His swing will show if he is about to play a high lob or a semi-lob.

You must judge the flight of the ball in its first twenty feet—that is, about half the distance from baseline to net. In this time, you must judge whether you can jump from your present position to smash or must run back.

BACKHAND AND FOREHAND DRIVE-VOLLEYS: This shot is so called because it is neither a volley nor a drive, but a combination of both, and this brings it into the smash category.

The shot is made with only about three-quarters of the backswing for the backhand or forehand drive and the racket is taken back rather more quickly. As for the full smash, the racket-head must be slightly closed. Otherwise, the ball will go out of court, high over the line. For the same reason, a full follow-through is essential.

To play the shot, the wrist should be turned and locked or the grip changed to ensure that the racket-head will be partly closed. The locked wrist is recommended because (a) there is little time to change the grip and (b) if the opponent returns your shot it might come back too fast to allow you to readjust your grip again, and you won't be able to handle his return.

BACKHAND SMASH: The racket is taken straight back, with the arm across the body and without any loop, which is impractical for this stroke. Bring the racket back over the left shoulder, watch the ball over your right. Never turn your back on the ball. To bring the racket forward to strike the ball, loop it in an arc.

This is an easy shot because it is a more natural movement than that for the forehand smash. It is much more comfortable to move the arm across the chest and throw it away than to take the arm away from the body and bring it forward. So don't be afraid of the backhand smash.

CAUSES OF MISSED SMASHES: A competent player should be able to hit his smashes into court all day long. The commonest causes of missed smashes are lack of confidence, the mistake of watching the opponent instead of the ball and the mistake of trying to do too much with the smash.

Confidence is an individual problem. A player can gain confidence in his smashing only by having a go until he has developed his technique to a point at which he can smash winners more or less at will.

The importance of 'having a go' is best demonstrated in the teaching methods of the Queensland coach, Charlie Hollis.

Charlie encourages his pupils very early in their instruction to go up boldly for their smashes. If they do this and duff the shots, he pats their heads and gently irons out the errors that caused the misses. If they leave the ground timidly and get the shot into court, he upbraids them. Better to try the right thing and fail than to succeed by compromise, he argues.

When Laver, then thirteen, appeared with the Brisbane *Courier-Mail* coaching school class in a demonstration before Harry Hopman, he 'climbed' to a great height for one smash which he put well over the base-line.

'He's a poor smasher,' Hopman commented.

'Poor smasher be darned!' said Charlie. 'He went up beautifully, and did you see the way he buried that ball? He killed it. There's plenty of time yet to teach him to keep them in court, as long as he keeps on going the right way about it.'

Trying to do too much with your smashes is a grievous error. Such mistakes include attempts to give the ball top-spin or back-spin, or to angle it too sharply to various parts of the court. Rely on smashing with a flat racket-face, as I have always done, making no effort to give the ball spin. In this way, you can concentrate on giving the ball power, speed and bounce for winners.

PLACEMENT TRICKS: You can hit a controlled smash to any part of the court. Position the left shoulder in the direction in which you wish to direct the ball and ensure that you have a full follow-through, and you can't miss. Without the follow-through, however, the ball is likely to go anywhere.

An exception to this rule is when you use the wrist to cut or twist the racket-face across the ball. This shot is not recommended for the average player, as it allows too little margin for error. The shot must be perfectly played if it is not to go into the net or out of court. Even for top-class players the safest smash placements are those played with great force with the full face of the racket.

Billy Sidwell hammers away a smash as team-mate Colin Long ducks low. On the other side of the net: great doubles combination Bill Talbert and Gar Mulloy, many times American doubles champions.

17 SINGLES STRATEGY
Adrian Quist

On tour in Australia in 1926, famous English cricketer Patsy Hendren played tennis with a thirteen-year-old Adelaide schoolboy. This was Adrian Quist, son of Karl Quist, the interstate cricketer with whom Hendren stayed. Hendren, skilled in several sports, was impressed with the boy and coaxed him to enter the South Australian schoolboys' championships with the promise that he could use two of Hendren's prized English rackets. Adrian was runner-up. His rise to tennis stardom had begun. He developed into a splendid stylist, a crafty, five-foot seven-inch all-court player gifted with speedy legs, who played some of the finest doubles tennis has seen. But this did not prevent him from building an imposing singles record. Quist played Davis Cup from 1933 to 1939, and in 1946 and 1948. His win over Bobby Riggs at Philadelphia in 1939 helped Australia regain the Davis Cup after a lapse of twenty years. Quist was Australian singles champion in 1936, 1940, 1948; New South Wales singles champion in 1935 and 1947; Victorian singles champion in 1935, 1936, 1938. He won ten straight Australian doubles titles—in 1936 and 1937 with his former Adelaide club-mate, Don Turnbull, and the next eight with John Bromwich. In 1935, he won the French and Wimbledon doubles with Crawford. He won Wimbledon again in 1950 with Bromwich, with whom he had taken the 1939 U.S. doubles. Quist today is an executive of the Dunlop Sports Company in Sydney, and is perhaps Australia's most authoritative writer and broadcaster on the game.

Once you have learned to hit the basic strokes over the net, the next step is to play competitive tennis. Whatever the level—school, club, district, interstate or international matches—you will never be a successful player unless you can repeat, in the stress of competition, the shots which work so well at practice.

The 1961 Italian Davis Cup team provided a classic example of what stress can do. This team of gifted players practised shots instead of playing tournaments in the lead-up to the challenge round, forgetting that you can do a lot with the ball at practice which is impossible under severe tension. The result was a debacle, with Australia overwhelming Italy.

You may be a tactical genius, a master of all shots, but if your nervous system will not permit you to use these assets, you are in trouble. There are players who, because of their physical and mental make-ups, are able to overcome the atmosphere of competition and raise their game to its highest pitch, but there are others who sink beneath the load and fail to play their natural game even in a social match.

The service is a major factor in the tactics of modern singles, but it is useless having a powerful service if you keep pounding the ball at your opponent's court without any thought. Do not give away the type of service you intend to make by the way you place your feet or by standing in a certain position behind the base-line. Take up your stance about two feet from the centre-line to keep your rival in two minds about whether you will serve down the centre or across court.

From the start of your competitive singles, you should continually rehearse the art of placing the ball just where you aim for. But you must play a game which is natural to you, whether this is to rely on volleying and a crushing net-attack, or an all-court game. Remember the cardinal tactical rule of lawn-tennis: there is a counter for every shot. However feeble your opponent makes you feel, keep searching for an answer to his onslaught.

We have heard a great deal in the last decade about the 'power' game, but I am at a loss to know what this catchword implies. I have followed international tennis since 1932 and I can assure you that the power net-rushers so prevalent today always have existed. Jean Borotra and Henri Cochet, of France, Wilmer Allison, Lester Stoefen and Joe Hunt, of the U.S.A., stormed the net with the same determination as Frank Sedgman, Lew Hoad, Pancho Gonzales and Tony Trabert.

If your game is best suited to base-line play, the first essential against opponents who storm the net is to control your emotions. Keep cool. Secondly, hit—don't steer—your passing shots, for the net-rusher always beats the man who pushes tentatively at the ball. There is enough room on the court for a crisp, well-timed drive to elude the incoming volleyer, who must rely partly on a threatening manner and on bustling you into errors.

Gottfried Von Cramm, the great German player, was never beaten by a net-rusher. He hit his ground-strokes with such perfect control and speed that to move to the net against him meant taking dangerous risks.

Here are some of the fundamental tactical approaches to good singles:

SETTING UP POINTS WITH SERVICE: Use your service to open up your opponent's court for winners, drawing your rival out of court with sliced, swerving or kicking deliveries wide to his body. For example, a sliced service about three-quarter way down the service court leaves an opponent with one of two returns to make: a drive down the line or across court. From either return, the server takes the initiative by punching his second shot deep to the opposite side of the court, the backhand wing, forcing the receiver to make an extremely precarious passing shot as the server moves to the net.

Neale Fraser watches the fate of an attempt to pass him by Rod Laver. Against an opponent who moves to the net as Fraser has done the other player must either lob over his head or pass on either side. The percentages favour the net rusher.

To open up your rival's court with service, first serves should be hit where shown in Figure 1, with flat or swerving deliveries. Second serves must have depth to keep him back and you should try to place swinging or kicking deliveries where shown in Figure 2.

Techniques of the net-rusher: eliminate the risk of angled passing shots by volleying down the centre (Figure 3) or direct your volleys to the backhand (Figure 4) for it is rare that your rival can consistently pass you on this side.

To elude opponents coming to the net you must either try for a passing shot off the return of service (Figure 5) or wait for an opportunity to do so in a rally. Success depends on concealing the direction of the shot until the last moment.

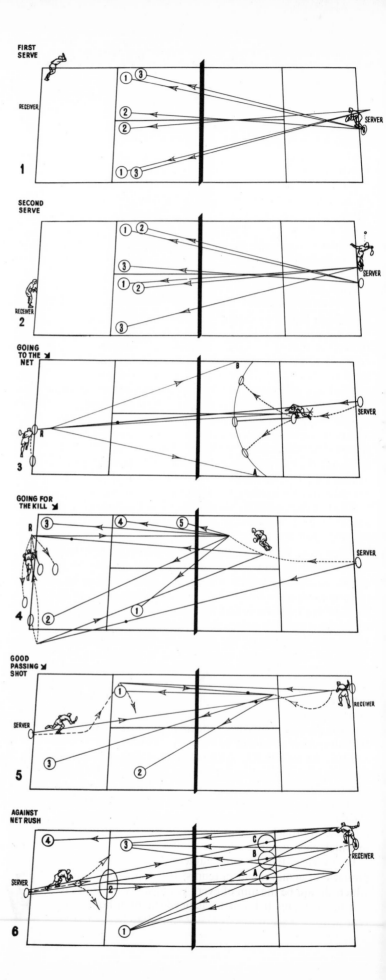

A net-rusher like Sedgman often swung his service wide to the forehand, but he countered the return by moving forward, and his wonderful anticipation and fast reflexes allowed him to volley to the open backhand court or straight down the line.

Jack Crawford was a master of the swinging service, but he was not a net-rusher. He planned the rally which started from his swinging serves and won many points in this way.

NET-ATTACK: If you are a net-rusher in the mould of recent champions, try the down-the-line theory, in which you play down the middle of the court, thus eliminating the risk of angled passing shots from your opponent.

The natural tendency of a volleyer is to direct his attack to the backhand court, gambling that his opponent will not possess the ability to hit consistently good backhand passing shots. But by attacking down the centre, the net-rusher moves in behind the line of flight and can if necessary step quickly to right or left. He should always remember that it is depth, not speed, which most disconcerts a base-liner. Never sacrifice length for speed, but, most of all, if you are passed a few times do not switch your attack by staying back and playing an unnatural game.

The secret of every great volleyer's success is his ability to sustain pressure and this can be done by other things than sheer blasting-power. Vary the pace of the approach-shot so that your rival does not get a chance to get his passing shots grooved. Don't get so close to the net that you are an easy target for a lob over your head.

BASE-LINE TECHNIQUES: The hall-mark of success in beating the net-rusher is to conceal the direction of your passing shots and to disguise until the last moment your intention of playing a lob. Keep the net-rusher guessing. It is possible to 'drift' a passing shot across court if the angle is perfect, but down-the-line passing shots must be hit firmly. After playing a passing shot, be ready to move in for the returns your rival mistimes, for often you can pick up a volley he has struggled to get and pass him on the next shot.

The lob is an invaluable shot and is one of the best counters to the net-rusher, but you must never become disheartened when some of your lobs are smashed away for winners. Those smashes may be taking a lot out of your opponents, and it is remarkable how a man who has put away a dozen smashes suddenly can start to miss the ball altogether or mishit it.

THE ALL-COURT APPROACH: The net-rusher spends about eighty-five per cent of his time in the fore-court cutting off drives, volleying, smashing; the base-liner remains pegged to the back of the court, stroking the ball deep to the corners; the all-court player combines all these approaches, adapting his tactics to suit the way in which each point is played.

In my view, the all-court game represents the highest pinnacle of achievement in tennis. It is a peak of control which should be the aim of every youngster who hopes to win major tennis titles or to achieve the high honour of representing his country in Davis Cup matches.

The all-court player relies on his driving pressure to produce short returns which he puts away at the net but in a non-bustling manner. Such a player has sufficient confidence in his own ability to take care of any situation, attacking his opponent's weaknesses behind powerful drives.

Players who can combine attack, defence, overheads and net-play do not have to risk all on a passing shot or on knocking off volleys at the net. They can plan their path to the net with deep, well-placed ground-shots, and when their opponents are struggling out of position, they can advance and dispatch their volleys for winners.

I think the greatest Davis Cup match in history was that between Von Cramm and Donald Budge at Wimbledon in 1937. For two sets Von Cramm threw every shot in the bag at Budge. His speed, placement and lack of errors would have shattered anyone but a great player like Budge, who gradually, through the excellence of his all-court game, earned a mighty victory. Donald Budge achieved that win by his control of every shot, and by his remarkably even temperament—attributes every youngster should seek. How sobering to reflect that despite all our international successes, Australia has produced very few all-court masters!

The types of services favoured in singles play depend on how the server positions the ball in the toss up. Throwing the ball straight up in front, the player serving can hit a powerful cannonball type shot. With the ball in the air to his right he must slice the serve, and with the ball to his left he produces a twist service.

18 MUSCLES, REFLEXES AND THE BIG STRETCH
Ashley Cooper

He was a fat boy with a brilliant scholastic record before he left his studies to concentrate on a tennis career that established him for a time as the world's No 1 amateur. Ashley John Cooper, born in Melbourne on 15 September 1936, was an outstanding junior before he won the 1956 Queensland singles by beating Rosewall in the semi-final and Hoad in the final. That same year he won the Australian hardcourt singles. In 1957 he was runner-up to Hoad at Wimbledon and to Anderson in the U.S. singles. By now Cooper had grown into a handsome, black-thatched figure with splendid ground-strokes and an inherent sense of good sportsmanship which crowds immediately appreciated. Like Tony Trabert and other top-line tennis players, he had trouble in achieving real speed, however, because of his naturally heavy legs. This caused him to do a lot of additional exercising to remain among the world's best, and it was not uncommon to see him come off the court after a hard match, don a track-suit and then run a few miles before he showered. This dedication won him a Davis Cup singles berth in 1957 and the 1958 Wimbledon title. Going down in the lift of a Queensland hotel, he met Miss Australia, Helen Wood. They fell in love and married the day after Cooper played in the 1958 Challenge Round at Brisbane. He turned professional immediately. Today, he is happy, prosperous—a condition he can attribute to his devotion to conditioning—although he has given up the life of the touring professional to concentrate on teaching.

I had just reached my first big championship final, the Australian championship at Kooyong, Melbourne, in January 1957. My opponent was Neale Fraser and Melbourne turned on one of its hottest days for the match. Inside the concrete bowl at Kooyong, the temperature hovered around 130 degrees and even the flies headed for the shade. But Neale and I were so evenly matched that it took us an hour and a half to play three sets, and when we came off for the break, the score was 6–3, 9–11, 6–4 in my favour. We came back for the fourth set, and somehow I sensed that Neale was very tired. This gave me enough confidence to rush through the fourth set 6–2 for the match. I am certain now that my superior fitness won that match and started me on the trail that led to the biggest title in tennis, Wimbledon. You may think I am a fitness crank, but I know I owe a lot of my tennis successes to the fact that I was just a little fitter than the other guy.

As a lad of fifteen, I had an idol, Frank Sedgman, who believed that physical fitness won matches. I was determined to follow in his footsteps, and I got to know the exercises Frank used as a junior in coaching classes conducted by Harry Hopman. I was a solidly built boy, to say the least. During the previous winter when I was only fourteen, I had been up around 14 stone 7 pounds, so I had to cut certain foods and really get to work with daily exercising.

The exercises 'Hop' showed me then had been used by

Using many exercises shown to him by Harry Hopman, Ashley Cooper achieved a peak of physical fitness which for a time established him as the world's number one amateur.

Australian Davis Cup teams for some years, and they are still used now. Generally, they are aimed at quickening the reflexes and building stamina.

Tennis is a game which repeatedly demands quick acceleration. You move only a few yards, but you have to cover the ground fast. So plodding slowly round and round an oval will not do much good unless you add speed work. Ken Rosewall is one of the fastest tennis-players I have ever seen, yet in a 100-yard sprint with other members of the Australian Davis Cup squad, he always ran last by a long margin. In ten-yard dashes, however, he always would be in front, and that's as far as you ever travel on a tennis-court.

My training always has included the following programme three or four times a week:
- I start off by warming up with three or four laps of the oval, just jogging and generally loosening the muscles (to rush straight into strenuous exercises or sudden halts and starts is a fine way of tearing a muscle).
- Properly warmed up, I then do several laps of wind-sprints, jogging for ten to fifteen yards and sprinting for the same distance at the fastest speed I can reach. I keep going until I can't do any more, and wind up with another couple of jogging laps. This is the letting-down, the unwinding, practised by all top athletes.

Of course, I did not do it this way on the first training spin. I started with a couple of jogging laps and about a dozen sprints—but that was enough to make me feel my feet and stomach had been torn out. I stuck at it, and after a few sessions, I found I could do thirty or forty sprints before I had to rest. About once a fortnight, I would go for a long run on the road to break the monotony of the oval, and would just keep on running and making short bursts until I couldn't go any further. After a couple of years of this, I found I would cover ten to twelve miles before I had to give up.

I suggest you take a look at yourself stripped before a mirror, and you will immediately see which areas you have to concentrate on when you are conditioning. Are your legs like mine, a little heavy? Or is that midriff a little bulky? Maybe the shoulders are stooped and lacking in power? Whatever your physical shortcomings, there are simple exercises for you which do not involve heavy outlay on equipment or gymnasium fees.

All the Australian Davis Cup players I have known have at some time done exercises like the following:

DOUBLE KNEE-JUMP (the 'kangaroo'): This takes time to learn, as balance plays an important part in it, but with a little perseverance you can become an expert at it. You simply leap into the air from a standing position, and at the peak of the jump you raise both knees until they touch your chest. Immediately you come down you repeat the process. Don Candy holds the record among all those who have been in Australia's great post-war Davis Cup squads with a total of ninety-three successive double knee-jumps. Frank Sedgman bet Candy he couldn't do eighty-five. Candy did them, but 'Sedg' said he hadn't made it—so Candy did another eight to prove his point. My best was around seventy, and most of the boys would be around that mark. When you are learning it's easier if you take a little steadying jump in between the leaps: it enables you to get your balance before you take off.

THE HIGH-MARK: This is simple for Australian Rules football addicts like me. From a squatting position, you leap as high as you can possibly go, returning to the squatting position.

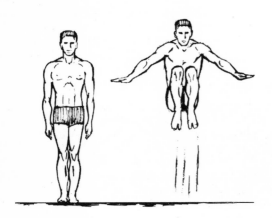

THE JACK-KNIFE: Jump upwards from a standing position, and at the peak height, throw the legs as far apart as possible and touch your toes with your hands. The legs are kept perfectly straight and are lifted as close up to the waist-line as you can get them. The jack-knife takes quite a time to master, and at first you will have to take a steadying jump in between the big leaps.

THE STAR JUMP: This consists of jumping from a standing position and flinging your arms and legs out at the peak to form a four-pointed star. Again, you need those steadying bounds at the start before you can expect to become an expert.

This type of exercise helps a lot in developing speed and agility on the court, as well as building your reserves of stamina, but almost any form of stretching exercise is good.

Twenty minutes of concentrated training is much better than an hour or more of exercising in a haphazard way.

I did twenty to thirty minutes really gruelling jumping and stretching exercises three or four times a week, and I always found that I got best results working out with a friend because we competed against each other.

Usually, those who do not do much conditioning feel the strain first in the stomach. There are a few simple stomach exercises that will prevent this. Harry Hopman once said to me: 'If you have strong and properly tuned stomach muscles, you will never feel exhausted in even the longest tennis matches.'

LEG-SCISSORS: Lying on your back, raise both legs about six inches from the floor and at the same time lift your upper body and prop yourself on your elbows. Then criss-cross your legs one above the other, and go back to the original position in fast scissor-movements. Alternate the scissoring so that first the right leg and then the left is the leg on top, and execute the whole thing as quickly as possible. Ensure that you anchor yourself with elbows and hands, or the whole thing will go awry.

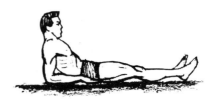

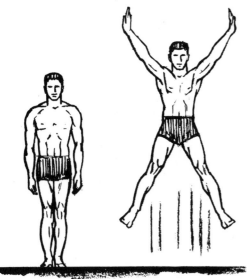

Here are some of the best stomach exercises:

LEG-RAISING: This is done lying on your back. You raise your legs until they are vertical, then return them almost to the starting position without allowing them to touch the floor, then take them back to the vertical position. Repeat until your stomach won't take it any more.

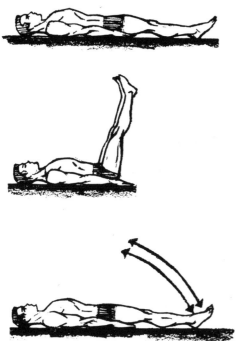

LEG-CIRCLING: Lying on your back, spread both arms out wide and raise your legs a few inches from the floor. Then start circling both legs to the left, and continue this in as big a circle as you can make. This exercise is done slowly, and you should try to make a bigger circle with each repetition. When your stomach starts to burn, take a rest, breathing in deeply—and then repeat the exercise, but this time turn to the right to make your circle.

THE PULL-UP: This is easy to explain, but tough to perform. Grab a bar, a branch of a tree or something similar so that you can hang in space. Then pull yourself up and chin the bar. Lower yourself back to the starting position without touching the ground, and repeat. Do as many as you can, even if it's only one at the start, and every time you do it try to increase the number.

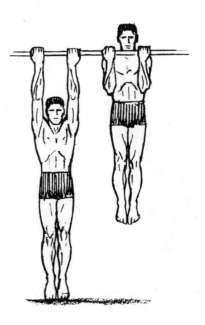

Next, we do the exercises for strengthening the arms and chest:

THE PRESS-UP: From a position on your stomach on the floor, push yourself up with your arms until they are perfectly straight. Keep your body-line straight throughout. At the peak height of the press, you should be balanced on hands and toes. If you are away out of trim, the press-up can be done at first by pushing up with the arms while keeping your knees on the floor. At the advanced stage, the press can be done with the hands spread in varying positions, from very wide apart to touching.

Always follow exercises like these with some stretching exercises so that your muscles do not become stiff or bulky. A tennis-player needs strength, but he also needs suppleness.

The exercises I have described do not include weights because I wanted to outline drills anyone can follow if they have a bare patch of land, and because I consider weight-lifting has to be carefully supervised. Indiscriminate use of weights will lead to heavy, bulky muscles and loss of co-ordination. For a tennis-player this is fatal.

Harry Hopman puts the 1961 Australian Davis Cup team through training at Kooyong, Melbourne. Strategy aside, Hopman got teams fitter than its members ever thought they could be. Often they neglect fitness when left to themselves.

19 TANTRUMS ARE FOR OPERA STARS
Alf Chave

Now in his sixties, he has been following big tennis since 1924. He played for Queensland from 1925 to 1939, and figured in the Queensland rankings for twenty-one years—1926 to 1947. Alf Chave was an all-court player who won two Queensland doubles titles, the first with Vivian McGrath, the second with John Bromwich. He has been a tennis broadcaster for the Australian Broadcasting Commission for thirty-two years, and has written on the game for the Brisbane Telegraph since 1930. Chave is a shrewd analyst of tournament matches, a cheery buoyant character to whom laughter comes easily. He is a highly successful fruit and produce merchant in Brisbane, Bundaberg and other towns—when he reaches for a phone in the Press-box one never knows if he is about to give a story to his paper or order another truckload of water-melons. In 1957, Chave refereed the Davis Cup inter-zone final between Belgium and the U.S. This was the match which hung on Herb Flam's inexplicable revival from near-collapse in the third set, a match which saw Chave exchange harsh words with the U.S. captain, Bill Talbert, about Flam's failure to return to the court inside the required ten minutes. Chave, who had fourteen years experience as manager of Queensland teams, was manager of the Australian's men's teams on world tours in 1961 and 1962.

There has never been a really great tennis-player who misbehaved regularly on the court. Some champions started off as problem players prone to tantrums, but they had to change their habits before they won important titles.

Tennis is traditionally a sport with high standards of conduct and fair play from both spectators and players, and therefore observance of the accepted courtesies becomes very important. Many of these practices will come naturally, as a reflection of your sense of fair play, but some will have to be learned. Try to get the reputation of being a courteous, friendly player, and people will be glad to have you on their courts. If you are playing without linesmen, you and your opponent will do the scoring. Give him your respect and don't contest his decisions, and he will do the same.

Aspiring young players should never forget the two essential aspects of bad court-behaviour. Firstly, it is in bad taste—the equivalent of insulting visitors to your home. Secondly, it never pays—the composed player wins every time. This does not mean a good player should not have any fire. Indeed, he must have it. He must love to play tennis, and deep in his heart he must hate to lose, but he must never show these things on the court. I felt very sorry for Tony Trabert the year he walked off the court in Sydney when the ageing John Bromwich led him two sets to love. I knew how futile Bromwich could make you feel, but here was a classic example of a player—disturbed by the crowd's one-sided applause for Bromwich—allowing his emotions to get the better of him. Frank

Bob Hewitt is particularly prone to displays of temperament when opponents needle him.

Sedgman and Ken McGregor in the days when they took Australia to the top of world amateur tennis were superb examples of sportsmanship and gentlemanly court demeanour. Of course, they hated to lose, but on the rare occasions when they did, they were gracious and full of praise for their conquerors.

Normally-well-behaved players can be needled into misconduct, of course, and since the war we have seen several top-liners who really excelled at the gentle art of gamesmanship. Bob Hewitt, who was in Australian teams I managed overseas, is particularly prone to displays of temperament when opponents needle him. His rivals know how easily Hewitt 'blows up', and he becomes a fairly frequent target for a spot of needling.

Tantrums can also be part of a player's tactical plan. Suzanne Lenglen once wept copiously when she dropped the second set of a match after having taken the first. Her opponent was so upset and sorry for Suzanne that she lost all concentration, and Suzanne won the third set without losing a game.

Many fine players have had their pattern of play scrambled like this. I saw Mervyn Rose play Mario Llamas one year in Italy and so break up Llamas's concentration that he could hardly get a ball back. Rose did it by stalling a bit, querying decisions, lecturing ball-boys—with a whole repertoire of dodges that made Llamas feel it was pointless to play.

The umpire had made several mistakes in Merv's favour. Rose just grinned.

Then the umpire, thoroughly bewildered by this succession of acts, worthy of a tennis Oscar, made a mistake against the Australian.

Rose called out, 'One more mistake and you are sacked.'

Bob Hewitt finishes among Wimbledon spectators in a 1962 match, declining to immediately get back to the court.

Warren Woodcock queries an umpire's ruling. The players concerned often are surprised at photos like this.

Two points later there was a close call. Rose looked at the umpire who immediately flung his excited Latin arms in the air, climbed from the stand and, like the Arab folding his tents, slunk off into the shadows.

Rose also played a notorious match in the Australian championships at White City, Sydney, in the Australian summer of 1957, against Warren Woodcock, no mean gamesman himself, which set off a furore of recriminations. Between them that day, they got through most of the chicanery known to tennis. They stalled each other, they sprawled full-length on the wet, bumpy court, they heckled umpire Frank Stewart, they called for rule-books, they halted play to instruct ball-boys in their duties. Rose served with one ball, and when it was faulted, held up play while he found another, a ploy that did nothing at all for Woodcock's concentration.

Gamesmanship and the Sephen Potter world of the secondary hamper have ensnared many players apart from Rose, for there is something in tennis that arouses the ham actor that lies just below the surface in most of us. I remember playing on a back court at Milton, Brisbane, one year and throwing my racket in the air in disgust over losing a point. The racket was never seen again, for it cleared the fence and was carried away in a storm-water canal behind it. I have heard how Count Salm, of Austria, squirted a soda-siphon at a dog whose bark annoyed him during a match—only to find the dog belonged to Suzanne Lenglen. I saw the blonde Czech giant, Roderick Menzel, in some of his celebrated burlesques. Menzel

complained of 'potato platz' courts when he missed shots, and once, in the final of the Italian championships, left the court—never to return—when spectators laughed at him (Menzel had dived full-length to retrieve a drop-shot from Palmiri, the Italian, had slipped and had become tangled in the net). When Menzel was on his Australian tour before the war, he protested over crying babies, called Kooyong a 'cow-paddock' and at Brisbane claimed a kookaburra in a tree was laughing at him (maybe it was), and asked for it to be removed. He called the Brisbane public 'a lot of wild cannibals'.

Nicholas Mishu, of Rumania, was a trick-serve specialist, likely to turn his back to the net to serve. The Dane, Torben Ulrich, used to play a clarinet in public telephone-boxes on the grounds of major courts—to soothe his nerves before a match, he claimed. Austrian Ferdie Huber would bite the ball and walk about the centre court on his hands, legs bent above him in the air. The American, Earl Cochell, used to sing or play left-handed, or spill water on opponents' racket-strings to upset their touch. One year at the French championships in Paris, Beppi Merlo towelled himself at the change-of-ends, fitted a fresh sweat-band on his wrist, strode to the base-line to receive service and began the search for his elusive grip for receiving service—which he made a practice of doing with the racket straight out in front, fingers nervously searching for the right grip. Well, this time Beppi's feet fidgeted and his head twitched from concentration, fingers spread out in the air. He had left his racket

98

beside the net-post! Tennis would be the poorer if it lacked characters like these. They provide it with a colour, a fascination, that dominates many club-house discussions. But I would not advise any youngster to set out to emulate them.

All of these people let spectators share their battle for control, but most of us have an inner struggle with our tempers. Jack Crawford is remembered throughout the tennis world for his impeccable court behaviour, but as one who played against Jack, I can assure you he had his problems like the rest of us. On the court, you could often hear him muttering beneath his breath over some missed shot or unfortunate decision. In the twenty-odd years I played against Jack I never did find out one word of what he mumbled. It could have been in Hindustani for all I know. What a contrast to Bob Hewitt who does his 'muttering' in a voice people in the first ten rows of the stand can hear!

Seldom in all the newspaper post-mortems of players' tantrums do sports-writers acknowledge the rights of the players. Umpires and linesmen can be wrong and often are. They can be sick, short-sighted or even go to sleep, and on a world tour you encounter some appalling decisions. Wimbledon, 1962 saw several unhappy incidents, and I was convinced this time that the umpires were more guilty than the players. Indeed, I have never known such arrogant umpires—little gods unable to admit they were wrong, even when spectators and both players agreed they were.

To be a top-class tennis-player you have to learn iron control of your nerves under the strain. Tantrums are for opera stars, not tennis-players, whatever the stress the big occasions throw up, and when your big moments come on the courts, you have to be mentally attuned for them. Adrian Quist gives a superb example of this in his account of how Vivian McGrath met a crucial test in a 1934 Davis Cup match in Prague against the Czech player Hecht, with the match poised at two rubbers all, and the winners to meet the U.S.A. at Wimbledon. Hecht won the first set amid wild screams of enthusiasm, and McGrath had to combat the wildly partisan gallery's all-out encouragement for Hecht. McGrath fought back to lead two sets to one, and in the fourth set, the crowd stood enmasse to cheer Hecht on each change of ends. As Hecht won points, he got roar after roar from spectators. McGrath had just his four Australian team-mates to cheer him on, but he never wavered, and he won the match. Aussies regularly group together at Continental tournaments to make sure that there is some applause for their own players. The Italians, who love to needle the opposition to effect an Italian win, got under Bob Hewitt's skin once and 'Lord Robert' yelled to me, 'Round up the boys, Chief.' We mustered about twenty Australians as a rival cheer squad and far from being upset the Italians laughed their heads off when we counter-barracked.

How comforting it would be to think that when your big chance arrives you will be as ready as McGrath was against Hecht. To do so, you need to practise good manners and the control of your emotions every time you take the court. The test of temperament in tennis is every bit as searching as the test of stroke-play.

The anguish of missing a shot you thought you should have got is universal but players express it in different ways. Here John Bromwich bows in annoyance.

20 THE LEFT-HANDED NONSENSE
Rod Laver

Rodney George Laver was born on 9 August 1938, at Rockhampton, Queensland, the freckled-skinned son of a right-handed farm manager who introduced Rod to tennis at the age of eight. At first, Rod's right-handed elder brothers dominated the court. Rod was not good enough to give them a hard game. But red-haired Rod persevered under coach Charlie Hollis, and when the family moved to Gladstone, he was getting his share of court-time. At thirteen, he was picked to play in the under-fourteen section of the Queensland age titles. Success here earned him a spot in the Queensland team which played New South Wales schoolboys in Sydney, where he stayed with the Hoad family. Dunlops gave him a job in Brisbane when he was fifteen, which enabled him to play regularly in tournaments, and two years later, he went around the world with Bob Mark under Harry Hopman's care in a threesome sponsored by a Tasmanian Lotteries tycoon. He won the U.S. junior singles and was runner-up in the French and Wimbledon junior tournaments. Back home, he won a string of junior titles around the Australian States, but did not really start to fulfil his rich promise until after his 1958 world tour. From here on, it was obvious that if he could add consistency to his brilliant, fluent stroke-play, he would prove a world-beater. Suddenly, his game settled on the right mixture, and in 1962, he became the second player to win the grand slam, the Australian, French, Wimbledon and U.S. singles in one year. Only Don Budge did it before him. Laver topped even Budge, however, when in 1969 he achieved the grand slam for the second time. When he lost in the quarter final to Roger Taylor in 1970 at Wimbledon he had won 31 straight matches in this tournament.

I don't like to play left-handers. The ball comes to me the wrong way round. I find that when I play a 'leftie' I'm always chasing my forehand, and the ball is always swinging in to my backhand. Usually, against right-handers it's the other way about, so I find it very awkward. I guess most people do, even right-handers, for in a way left-handers are the oddballs of tennis. I always have had to concentrate a little harder against left-handers like Neale Fraser or Mervyn Rose. It often takes several games before I get my game grooved to their style.

I've heard that when Ken Rosewall was a kid he was a natural left-hander who wrote, threw and swung a bat left-handed. His father, a Sydney district player, considered that, because he was a 'leftie', Ken would have no chance of succeeding in tennis so he switched Ken to right-handed tennis. Even now Ken plays golf left-handed.

Probably, what Ken's father had in mind was the left-hander's old bugbear: the weakness of the sliced backhand. I haven't been in big tennis for long, but of the top-class left-handers I've known Jaroslav Drobny, Tappy Larsen, Mervyn Rose and Neale Fraser, were all supposed to have this backhand weakness. But if you are a left-hander like them you can console yourself with the fact that 'lefties' have some big weapons to compensate for their suspect backhands. They have a big advantage when serving, for example, as they can swing the ball away much more sharply than right-handers. And the left-hander's forehand usually carries naturally heavy top-spin, with a lot of wrist in the shot. Drobny, Larsen, Rose and Fraser all had swinging services which right-handers found swung awkwardly away from them or into their bodies.

In social and district tennis, the left-hander's strengths —service and forehand—probably will bring their share of success. In the higher classes of tennis, left-handers have to get used to receiving plenty of lobs directed over their right shoulders. Few left-handers can do much with a backhand smash, and this often seems to me to be a bigger weakness than the traditional backhand woes. You can do something about the backhands: through hard practice you can learn to hit it flat or with top-spin. But it is darned difficult to reach the ball high above your right shoulder. The best defence is speed, which enables you to move to the right under the ball.

But the problem is not as worrying as it may sound because very few lobs are hit exactly as your opponent wishes. You get a lot of high ones intended to pass over your right shoulder, which are just right for smashing away for winners. And, brother, when a left-hander smashes, he almost always does so with heaps of angle on the ball, mostly down the left-hand side of the opposite court.

If my backhand is not weak, then how do I play it? Well, I hold my right hand on the racket as a sort of guide until the ball nears and I have the shot lined up. I stroke the ball flat with my fingers in a left-hander's Eastern grip, locking the wrist at the moment of impact and not squeezing the racket in too close to the body. Few left-

Rod Laver's forehand carries naturally heavy top-spin with a lot of wrist in the shot.

handers can impart the backhand top-spin I can get by rolling the racket over the ball. For years I played what I call 'fun tennis', experimenting with shots. I was never consistent for more than a few games, but I loved trying something new and going for the impossible shot. Now it's all melted down to a game I think I can control. Probably, a lot of the shots I play today are the result of all that experimenting.

Left-handers can be very effective in doubles, and although I have never had a regular partner, I won the last three Australian amateur doubles titles in which I played—one with Roy Emerson and two with Bob Mark. Left-handers like Rose and Fraser built up a splendid record in doubles.

The game of doubles, as Colin Long says in his chapter of this book, demands different shots from singles, and many of these doubles shots are particularly suited to the left-handed game. Left-handers have an effective doubles serve, a fast forehand return of service and can use the chip across the body. They don't often have trouble learning to volley, and their looped forehand lob is also very useful in doubles.

Partly because they get so much swerve and spin on the ball, left-handers do well on courts which are a little damp or on which the grass has been allowed to grow a little long. I could always do things with the ball at Forest Hills which I couldn't do at Wimbledon or the hard surfaces in Australia. The reason was that the grass on which we played the U.S. singles was longer and gave the spin I applied to the ball more chance to work.

Night matches never worry me because they are played either on wood or on grass which is just a little damp with dew. This means I feel I can control the ball more

easily. Similarly, the loose continental clay courts help me a bit, especially Roland Garros, where they play the French championships.

In my grand-slam of all four major singles in one year, I reckon I went closest to losing in Paris, where three players had great chances of beating me. Martin Mulligan and Neale Fraser had match-points against me, and Roy Emerson had me in lots of trouble, but at the crucial moments I just seemed able to play a great shot or a flukey one that they couldn't do anything with. In some tournaments, you just feel fate wants you to win, and for me, Paris, 1963, was certainly one of those.

The last few days of Forest Hills, when I just needed the U.S. title for a full hand, were a terrific strain. I don't suffer from nerves normally, but there was so much stuff in the papers about me and my left-hander's attack, and about whether I could do it and whether I was as good as Budge, that I got pretty tense. I was lucky that Emerson was not in his very best form in the final and that I was right on my game. You have to have luck to win the grand slam.

Anyway, let's hope that my success in making the grand-slam will encourage young left-handers to go on. As I have said, left-handers have some tremendous natural advantages, and if they work on the well-known left-handers' weaknesses on the backhand and overhead, there is no title they cannot win. The secret lies in learning to hit a good, flat backhand drive, and on the highest levels of the game, in being able to hit that backhand with top-spin. I was given a guarantee of $110,000 late in 1962 to turn professional, which demonstrates how worthwhile the effort of acquiring these shots can be. If you are a 'leftie', I hope you are as lucky as I have been.

Rod Laver's supreme control of spin has lifted him above many of his contemporaries, but his great mobility—clearly shown in this shot—should not be forgotten.

Neale Fraser stretches for a wide backhand return. With a game built on service power, mobility and fighting spirit, he overcame the traditional left-handers' groundshot weakness.

21 DOUBLES TACTICS
Colin Long

In 1937, a talented all-round schoolboy sportsman beat Harry Hopman in the first round of the Melbourne Cricket Club's first senior-junior championships. Next day, the boy's headmaster at Melbourne Grammar School called him in and instructed him to drop tennis and concentrate on cricket and football—sports at which the boy excelled. Colin Long knew then that tennis was the sport he preferred. That year, he made the Victorian senior team which competed in interstate events. War came before he could fulfil Davis Cup ambitions and Long served for five years with the A.I.F. He was twenty-eight when he was chosen in the 1946 Australian team for the Cup. Long was a heavily built man who is remembered around the world's major tennis arenas for thrilling, ball-pounding, high-leaping doubles thrillers. In 1947, Long and Bromwich beat Drobny and Cernik in the Davis Cup inter-zone final, and then defeated Kramer and Schroeder in four sets—Australia's only challenge round win that year. Long and Nancye Bolton won the Australian mixed doubles in 1940, 1946, 1947 and 1948. Long won the 1946 Victorian doubles with Bromwich, and was runner-up in the 1948 Australian doubles with Sedgman, the year they won the South Australian doubles. Long today works in sales promotion and occasionally as a television sports commentator.

Not enough players who enter important doubles events today bother to learn much about the tactics of this fascinating phase of tennis. Often as I watch doubles these days, I sadden over the lack of science, the failure of the players to realise that doubles demands a completely different approach to stroke-making from singles. And yet Australian tennis has a great doubles heritage, and if you rifle through the record books, you will find dozens of pairs who gained international distinction—pairs as good as any in the world at their prime: Brookes-Wilding, Patterson-Hawkes, Hopman-Crawford, Quist-Turnbull, Bromwich-Quist, Sedgman-McGregor, Hoad-Rosewall, Fraser-Emerson, Stolle-Hewitt—the list seems endless. Ten of the first sixteen Wimbledon doubles titles after the World War II were won by Australians. All of these men understood the basic issue that doubles is a team game and that for fifty per cent of the time in doubles you should try to set up winners for your partner.

The doubles game presents problems quite different from singles. The tactics are more varied, and the moves are more complicated. It is not true that in doubles 'a player has only half the court to cover'. The secret of doubles play is in the team-work which players bring to it: they must cover the whole court together. Jack Kramer, one of the all-time greats in singles, once told me he concentrated so much on singles he lost the art of doubles, especially the trick of returning to your opponent's feet.

The first essential, of course, is to choose the correct partner. Bromwich and Quist were a champion pair, but Quist and Hopman didn't click. McGregor was fair when paired with other top-liners, but with Sedgman, McGregor was the superb foil. Choice of partner depends on whether your game complements that of the man with whom you wish to play—and whether he has the ability to play the vital doubles shots well. Dinny Pails in his amateur days was a very successful singles player, but in doubles his failure to punch his first volley was disastrous, and his doubles record remained poor.

I never thought that Hoad and Rosewall, in their amateur days, were a really great doubles pair. Rosewall lacked the essential skill overhead at that stage of his development, and this led to the Australian Davis Cup selectors separating them for the 1953 challenge round when the selectors' preference for Rex Hartwig as Hoad's partner caused a national furore. Hoad and Rosewall succeeded in doubles, despite Rosewall's vulnerability overhead, largely because they were exponents of the aggressive tactics perfected by Bromwich and Quist, who probably established the pattern of the Australian pairs that followed them. Australians usually serve well, but the key to the Bromwich-Quist method was to return service well, and move in quickly to volley the next shot.

Doubles is a game of reflexes. Everything is probing and speed. It will help your singles a great deal if you give doubles the attention it deserves. When Harry Hopman was training his teams frequently there would be two players or more on one side of the net pounding the ball at a single player on the other side. This system sharpened the reflexes to a pitch where most players in Hopman's teams automatically were workmanlike doubles players.

Here are the fundamental points to learn if you wish to succeed in doubles:

Tony Roche and John Newcombe, one of the greatest doubles combinations in the world.

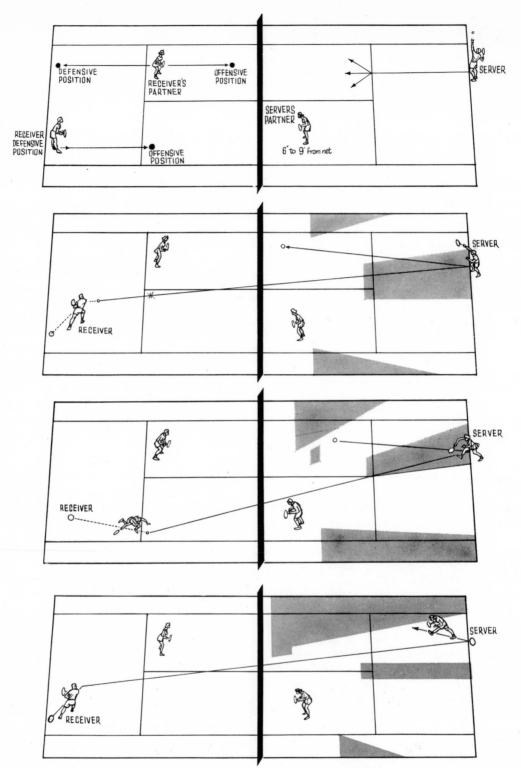

1. This sketch shows normal positions for serving. The server stands midway between the sideline and the centreline. The server's partner stands 6 ft. to 9 ft. from the net and about 1 ft. from the sideline. The receiver stands just inside the baseline, his partner just inside the service court. For beginners, the receiver's partner can retire to baseline.

2. To return a **good** service, the receiver should aim for the shaded areas, trying for outright winners in the smaller areas or to set up a chance for his partner to volley by returning to the server's feet.

3. Returning a **bad** service, the receiver should direct the ball to any of the shaded areas. In any of the larger shaded areas, winners or forced errors probably may result. In the tiny area, the server will have to take the ball at the feet.

4. A good service wasted by the server's failure to follow it to the net. By hanging back, the server gives the receiver a chance to return it to any of the shaded areas, all of which will present problems.

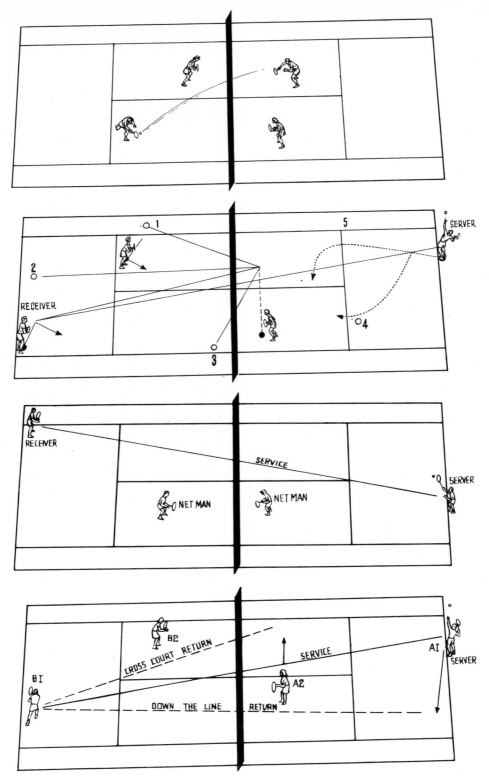

5. Winning doubles demands that all four players should get to the net often, with the team that gets to the all important rising ball, hitting down on it for a winner or for a forced error.

6. The intercept: This is made by the net man when a strong serve by his partner has drawn a weak return. The server comes up path 4 on a signalled "poach" or up path 5 on an unsignalled poach. Spots marked 1, 2 and 3 show possible placements of interceptor's volley.

8. SCISSORS: This is a shock technique in which the server and his partner change sides immediately after the serve is hit. It brings rich dividends when the net player is a strong volleyer, quick to intercept.

7. TANDEM: Serving to a player who has difficulty hitting down the line, the server and his partner stand on the same side of the court. It's a tactic to use occasionally to break up the receiver's rhythm and confidence.

WORK FOR YOUR PARTNER: Often if you return an opponent's service right at his feet, your partner will win the point by hammering away the return. When you return service, you must keep the ball low, forcing opponents into making defensive returns. Your partner will then capitalize with volleying interceptions or smashes.

ALWAYS REMEMBER IT IS A CRIME TO SERVE DOUBLE FAULTS: Missing with your first service is bad enough in singles, but in doubles you should try to get ninety per cent of your first services in. It's far better to play at controlled three-quarter pace with attention to accuracy—as it puts you on the attack—than to try for cannonball services. When you miss your first service against a good pair they will automatically move in closer to the net to take your second service, and this puts you on the defensive or worries you into error on your second service.

NEVER MISS A RETURN OF SERVICE: This is the great secret of successful doubles, and no pair ever taught me the truth of it more than Bromwich and Quist. I have seen Bromwich in a doubles against Donald Budge and Gene Mako go through an entire match without missing a return of service—or so it seemed! Today, that would be hailed as incredible. Psychologically, a player who always get his returns of service back into play has a great advantage. Hit-and-miss returns provide odd spectacular winners, but seldom win matches.

Bromwich and Quist created a service worry for their opponents, for always in the back of your mind you had the nagging certainty that you would have to play a great volley or a fine passing shot after your service—they would undoubtedly get your service back. This left you with the uncanny feeling that Bromwich and Quist always knew what you were about to do.

DON'T TRY FOR CLEVER ANGLES OR 'DINK' VOLLEYS UNTIL YOU HAVE PERFECTED THE DOWN-THE-CENTRE VOLLEY: Angles and dinks are selfish, individualist shots. Your opening volley should always be down the centre. This way, the angles disappear for your opponents, and often this forces your rivals into error. Indeed, the volley down the centre is one of the fundamentals of good doubles.

ANY SHOT YOU GET ABOVE THE LEVEL OF THE NET INSIDE THE SERVICE COURT MUST BE PUNCHED: If you are in as close as that, it is essential that you attack. But keep calm near the net. Don't go wild just because you sense a winner. A ball over the level of your shoulder deserves to be smashed away for a winner. A powerful smash is the elixir of tennis—enjoy it!

NEVER THINK OF THE LOB AS A DEFENSIVE SHOT: Get it into your mind that the lob is a point-winner. Practise the lob as you do the rest of your strokes.

One of the greatest doubles pairings of all time, 'Little Bill' Johnston and 'Big Bill' Tilden in action at Wimbledon, with Johnston about to volley. Tilden's alertness is admirable.

And if you want to study a first-rate attacking lob, admirably disguised, watch Rod Laver play the shot. I once saw Ken McGregor put up ten lobs in a few games to Frank Sedgman. They were gems. Sedgman, unable to cope with perfect-length tosses, lost command of the net, and his entire game lost its attack and purpose. Result: Ken McGregor surprised the tennis world defeating Sedgman in that 1952 Australian singles final.

WATCH THE SIDE-LINE WHEN YOUR PARTNER HITS A GOOD SHOT: There is a tendency among young players to crowd the centre on attack. This is dangerous, because often the man receiving a ball low and wide can only return down the side-line.

LEARN TO 'CROWD': Never allow your opponents time to settle, relax or adjust their game to the pace that suits them. Learn to 'threaten'. Move closer to the net at the slightest opportunity, thus putting pressure on your rivals. Make the match mentally demanding for them. Never allow your opponents to think you are mechanical. Give them plenty of variation. Stop their net-man from thinking he can chop off all your returns by hitting one or two down the side-lines. Part of this 'crowding' and 'threatening' is to hit down at your rivals' feet—never to the baseline.

And now a couple of queries on tactics:

TANDEM This is a stratagem designed to cut off a favourite cross-court return from a doubles opponent. It forces the player to return down the line, an unusual service return in doubles, and therefore often badly played. Playing tandem, you and your partner stand on the same side of the court, inviting your rivals to hit the ball into the vacant half of the court, with the server moving across to cover the open territory.

One of the best displays of the crafty use of tandem formation came at the 1958 Challenge Round at Brisbane when the American pair, Alex Olmedo and Ham Richardson, ran into a lot of trouble against Australia's Anderson and Fraser. In the first three sets—all of which Australia, 2–1 at the interval, could have won—Fraser hit some brilliant cross-court backhand returns. Up in the television commentary boxes, world-champion professional Pancho Gonzales noticed that Fraser very seldom hit his backhand return down the line. Indeed, he played the shot with a confined swing which made it difficult to hit it down the line. So, at the break between the third and fourth sets, Gonzales sent a message to the Americans recommending that they use the tandem formation on Fraser. Richardson and Olmedo proceeded to do this with striking effect. They did not adopt the tandem formation every time either one served to Fraser, nor did they serve every ball to his backhand. But they would use the tandem formation for two points in a row and then not for several points, all the time keeping the Australians guessing and upsetting the rhythm of Fraser's stroking. Finding two men on one side of the court ready to take his favourite cross-court backhand, Fraser lost rhythm, then lost confidence and had great difficulty getting the ball back into play anywhere in the vacant side of the court. He had played brilliantly in the first three sets, carrying a badly out-of-touch Anderson, but now his game started to disintegrate.

SCISSORS This is a technique in which the net-man anticipates and moves to cover the cross-court return, with the server moving quickly to cover the down-the-line return. This move calls for split-second timing—and needs plenty of practice before being put into force.

The most brilliant individual doubles display I ever saw was by the Australian two-hander, Geoff. Brown, when I partnered him in a 1948 Davis Cup tie in Mexico City against the Mexicans, Gustavo Palafox and Armando Vega. Brown hit the ball with incredible power, often with both feet off the ground. In the first game, he blasted four winners for us to take the game to love, and he kept it up for the first eight games before I lost my service. Brown thus demoralized two good players on their home court, and we won 6–0, 6–2. Even the partisan Mexican crowd gasped and applauded Brown. Not all players can sustain the standard of power doubles Geoff. Brown played that day in Mexico, but if you apply yourself to the basic techniques of doubles you can savour the thrill of it for a few games at least—and open up a fascinating new part of tennis for yourself.

Rod Laver, left, drops back to help partner Bob Mark as Mark leaps high to try to reach an overhead.

22 THE RULES—STUDY THESE POINTS
Cliff Sproule

Clifford Ewing Sproule, son of a schoolteacher, started playing tennis at the age of ten in 1915 on concrete public courts in Balgownie, south of Sydney. Cliff developed a quiet, subtle game and won the South Coast junior and senior singles and two country carnival singles. In 1926, he played in the New South Wales Linton Cup team with Jack Crawford and Harry Hopman. He reached the finals of the national junior singles and doubles that year, losing the singles to Crawford and the doubles, with J. O. Sherwood, to Crawford and Hopman. He played for Australia against Japan in 1932. In 1933, Sproule led world champion Ellie Vines 7–5, 7–5, 5–1 and 40–30, but lost in five sets in the Victorian championships. He retired from tennis in 1934 to concentrate on his job with the Commonwealth Bank, for which he is now branch liaison officer. As a tennis administrator, Sproule has few peers. He was non-playing captain of the 1936–37 Davis Cup teams, managed the Australian 1949 Davis Cup team and touring teams in 1956 and 1957. Sproule has been an Australian selector for three decades and the referee of ten successive Challenge Rounds in Australia from 1951. By his shrewdness and knowledge of the rules he has built a world-wide reputation for the excellence of his refereeing.

At the 1960 Challenge Round in Sydney, Italian Nicola Pietrangeli won the toss before the start of his singles against Rod Laver. There, for the first time in all my Davis Cup experience, I saw a player throw away the right to serve first as Pietrangeli chose the southern end of the court. 'What do I do now, "Hop"?' Laver asked Harry Hopman. Then, after an earnest discussion with 'Hop', Laver walked to the northern end to serve. Italian hopes of taking advantage of Laver's normally slow start had mis-fired. By choosing the southern end, Pietrangeli had forfeited the right, which winning the toss carries, of choosing whether he would serve or receive service, and had thus ruined the Italian plan that, by serving first, he might run to a 3–0 lead before Laver settled down.

When you toss at the start of a tennis-match what are you tossing for? Well, you toss for one of three things: the right to serve first, or the right to receive service, or the right to select the end you prefer. You cannot choose the end you want and retain the right to ask your rival to receive or serve—he then has that right. If you elect to receive service, your rival has the choice of ends as well as the right to serve.

Very few tennis players, even those who appear in Wimbledon finals and in Davis Cup challenge rounds, fully understand all the rules of the game. While refereeing ten challenge rounds, I have seen many examples like that of Pietrangeli which demonstrated that the players were not fully aware of their rights, or of those of their opponents. Most champion players cite instances when

they lost crucial points through ignorance of the rules—and some can even tell of matches lost because of it. And if this applies to famous players then how much more unaware of the rules are spectators?

One rule the tennis public does not appreciate is that an umpire cannot over-rule a linesman's decision. The referee cannot over-rule the linesman, either, but he can remove a linesman on appeal.

If a ball is unsighted, the linesman should stand up and place his hand over his eyes. Then the umpire is allowed to take over the call if he is properly placed to do so. If the umpire is not positioned to make the call, he should play a 'let'. When a linesman realizes he has made an incorrect call and stands to call 'correction', the umpire must play a 'let'.

One of the fascinations of tennis, however, is that incidents continue to arise which are difficult to arbitrate on from the rule-book. There was one Challenge Round in which the centre strap came out of its attachment on the court. I allowed a 'let', as during the rally the ball had hit the net-cord and bounced over and, as a result, the net might have been higher than permitted. The ruling would have been a very contentious one had the Davis Cup rested on that point.

I suppose I have had my share of incidents, too, over whether players could wear spikes. Some players consider all referees are opposed to spikes, but this is not true. You have to consider the condition of the court and the effect spikes will have on the playing surface for later matches. At the 1958 Challenge Round in Brisbane, spikes were worn on all three days and had less effect on the court than ordinary tennis-shoes. At the 1953 Melbourne Challenge Round, America's Tony Trabert, down a set

Harry Hopman instructs Lew Hoad.

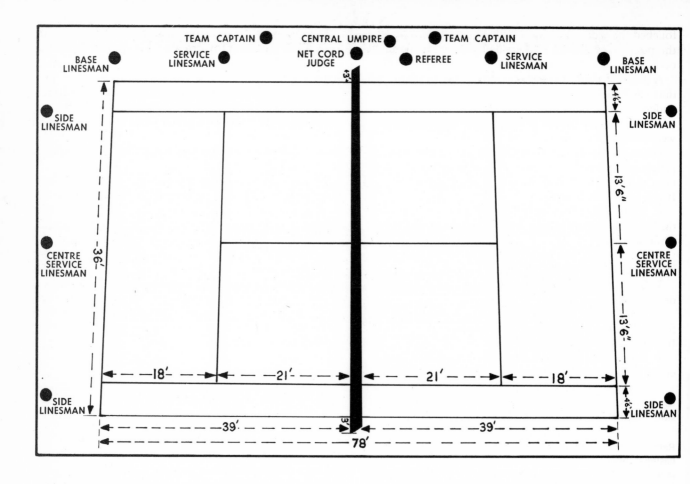

Diagram shows dimensions of a tennis court and the positions of officials for a Davis Cup match. Unhappily few events can raise this lineup.

and 2–3 to Lew Hoad, asked me if he could wear spikes. I disallowed this because the court had been baked hard in the sun and had some bare patches around the baseline. I believed spikes would have lifted these and made the bounce of the ball most uncertain. The Americans' reaction to my decision was hostile. About fifteen minutes later, I allowed spikes, and this again puzzled them, but by then the cracks had been sealed by light drizzle.

The use of spikes has to be requested by the players. If one player has spikes and his rival hasn't, this does not prevent the man with spikes being allowed to wear them. The referee expects grass-court tournament players to have spikes as part of their gear. Before each Challenge Round, I always inspect the players' spikes in the dressing-rooms to ensure that the spikes are blunt, no more than the regulation three-eighths of an inch long, and that there are spikes on the heel as well as the sole.

American Lev Richards made one of the fairest Davis Cup decisions when he refereed the Challenge Round match between Australia and America in 1959. Rain fell in the match between Fraser and MacKay, and the light was failing when Richards halted the match at two-sets all. The light apparently was good enough to have played one or two more games, but this could only have given one side an advantage. By stopping the match then, Richards left all the final set for the next day. This meant that Richards had adhered to the principles all referees should follow: (1) to be fair, come what may, and (2) never to give one side an advantage at the expense of the other. When services are being held alternately, it's preferable that appeals against the light should be allowed only when the scores are level.

It should be every young player's aim at the start of his career never to take an unfair advantage of an opponent, but not to concede one foolishly either, because of ignorance of the rules. Play your tennis to the rule-book, and you will get infinitely more satisfaction from it. This particularly applies when you consider conceding a point after your opponent has had a bad call. Throwing him a point doesn't make up for a bad call, because the state of the game has changed. Always play to the umpire's call, irrespective of the justice handed out, for these things have a way of balancing themselves.

Australia and all the nations affiliated to the International Lawn Tennis Federation play under the rules of the I.L.T.F., which has special regulations for Davis Cup competitions. The official rule-book is available from all State associations in Australia. For aspiring players it can be a mesmerizing document. For instance, page 32 raises the question: In serving, the racket flies from the server's hand and touches the net before the ball has touched the ground. Is this a fault or does the server lose the point? The answer is that the server loses the point because his racket touches the net while the ball is in play.

A player is permitted to lean over the net to play a ball that has bounced backwards, but he cannot put his feet underneath the net to play the ball before it has passed over the net; nor can he touch the net with anything he wears or carries without losing the point.

What is a foot fault? Today, many young players completely disregard the foot fault rule, although it has never been clearer than it is now. Under the present rule:
It is a foot fault if you:

1. Stand with a foot on the base-line (or move it on to the base-line) before hitting the ball, or on hitting the ball, while serving.

2. Move either foot into the court (to touch the ground inside the court area) before hitting the ball when serving.

3. Stand with a foot across or beyond the centre-mark or the side-line.

4. After taking up your stance, take a deliberate step forward before hitting the ball in service.
It is not a foot fault if you:

1. Jump into the air with both feet off the ground either before or when hitting the ball in service.

2. Swing your foot over the base-line (but not touching the ground inside the court area), the centre-line or the side-line, before or when hitting the ball in service.

3. Jump over the base-line toward the net with both feet off the ground (provided that you do not touch the ground inside the court area before hitting the ball) when delivering the service.

Today's rule book, painstakingly revised and polished to get it to its easily understood form, has a lot to say about the implements with which we play tennis. One of the most important of these is the ball itself which has been standardized around the world through the efforts of the I.L.T.F.

We look on standardized tennis-ball pressures, cloth covering and measured performances in bound-tests as normal, but until the 1930s, when the I.L.T.F. set up a standards committee, there was no international standard for these. In Victoria, for the first few years after the introduction of the game, the balls used were uncovered, while those used in New South Wales were the English type, covered by cloth. The Englishman, Dr W.V. Eaves, on his second visit to Australia in 1902, expressed such contempt for the 'uncovered abomination' used in Victoria that it caused the covered ball to become standard in interstate matches.

Here are some of the points in the rule book which most frequently cause discussion:

FOUL SHOT: If a ball is struck twice or intercepted before it passes over the net, or a player touches it in any way while the ball is in play, or a ball in play touches anything

Referee Cliff Sproule watches as Tony Trabert adjusts tape on blistered fingers. U.S. captain Bill Talbert, back to camera, prepares the tape for Trabert. The referee has to be satisfied breaks like this are genuine and don't constitute deliberate stalling.

Team captain Harry Hopman adjusts Neale Fraser's socks during the 1962 Challenge Round at Brisbane. Spiked shoes, always a contentious subject among players, were worn throughout the tie.

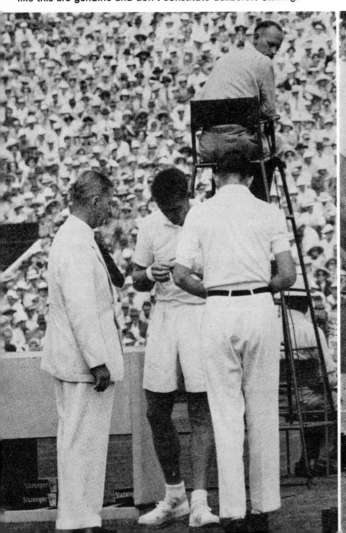

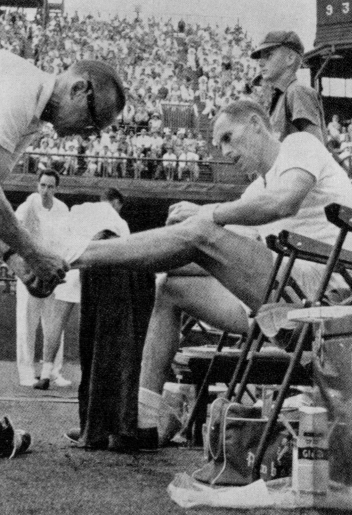

a player wears or carries, the umpire should call, 'foul stroke'. I always like to see youngsters admit to 'foul strokes', for the player knows best if it has grazed his racket or touched his clothing, or whether he has failed to get it up.

GOOD SHOT: The ball in singles can strike the net-post and go in and be allowed, although the singles posts are outside the singles side-lines. If you are playing singles with doubles posts up and the ball hits the post and goes in, the shot is not good because the doubles post is outside the singles court.

CLASH OF RACKETS: Only one racket may strike the ball—even though the other racket may come up from behind it and supply impetus. However, if both rackets touch the ball, it is a foul shot.

PUFFS OF CHALK: You can raise the chalk with a shot, and the shot can still be out. The lines may have been trampled over and the chalk raised and spread outside the line.

HITTING ROUND THE NET-POST: If the ball is returned outside the net-post, either above or below the level of the top of the net, even though it may touch the post, it is a good shot, provided it hits the ground within the proper court.

BALL ON THE COURT: Whose point is it if a player making a good return hits a spare ball lying on the court? The rule says the point goes to the striker if the correct ball is not returned. It is a player's responsibility to remove the ball from his side of the court. Apart from the fact that it could cost you the point, it is unwise to leave the first ball on the court after serving your second as it could cause an accident.

SERVER CATCHING THE BALL: After throwing the ball up to serve, the server decides not to strike it and catches it instead. Is it a fault? No, not unless the server strikes at the ball and misses it.

SERVICE THAT HITS A POST: In serving in a singles match played on a doubles court with doubles and singles net-posts, the ball hits a singles post and hits the ground within the lines on the right side of the court. Is this a fault or a let? In serving it is a fault, but it would be allowed in general play. For the service, the singles post, the doubles post and the portion of net, the strap and the band between them are permanent fixtures.

RACKET OVER THE NET: In making a volley, a player swings his racket over the net without touching it. Is his return good? Yes, provided the ball has passed the net before he made his stroke.

INTERFERENCE WITH A PLAYER: When there is interference such as another ball, paper, dog, cat or spectator coming on to the court, the entire point should be replayed. If the first service is a fault and the interference occurs during the rally following the second service, two services must be allowed. It is worth remembering here, incidentally, that the two-service rule was originally introduced to make the game more attractive to women!

One of the most intriguing moments in my career as a referee came during the 1958 Brisbane Davis Cup Challenge Round when a linesman, apparently over-excited by the tension in a dramatic doubles, involuntarily threw out his hand as Alex Olmedo followed his serve to the net to volley. Olmedo netted the volley and his partner, Ham Richardson, then asked for the point to be replayed, arguing that the linesman's arm waving had upset Olmedo. I over-ruled this because I was convinced Olmedo had not seen the arm go out, which was shown by the fact that Olmedo immediately moved to the other side of the court to serve. In any case, Richardson had no right to ask for the point to be replayed; that was up to Olmedo.

On the next day of that very exciting Challenge Round, Olmedo walked over to the umpire's chair to get a towel to clean his racket-handle midway through a game. He did it several times, and finally I intervened, for the only time a player is permitted to do this is at the change of ends or at the end of a set.

Stalling by players is one of the most difficult problems a referee faces. The player is not allowed to take any rest on the plea of excessive heat or slippery grips other than the specified ten minutes after the third set. The continuous-play rule applies even when a player is stricken with cramp. The rules acknowledge that cramps are due to muscle fatigue and that therefore there should be no suspension of play if one player has an attack. He must play or forfeit.

Young players starting on their competitive careers should always remember it is their responsibility to turn up on time ready to play. The rules say you can be disqualified for being late but no tournament organizer likes to act on this rule. You will rid him of one of his biggest worries if you are punctual. Remember, too, that you owe respect to tournament officials who devote their leisure without pay to conducting the matches.

Among rules often puzzling to novices are those that (a) permit shots to be returned around the net post, (b) bring footfaults through creeping over the baseline or by misunderstanding the "swing foot" rule, (c) describe how points are won or lost through doubles partners' rackets clashing.

AROUND THE NET POST

NEW AND OLD
RULE COMPARISON ▶

BASELINE
FORGOTTEN

CLASHING ▶
RACQUETS

23 TENNIS FOR THE MIDDLE-AGED
Ian Ayre

Ian Ayre, thirty-three, after a notable playing career which put him in the Australian Davis Cup team in 1951 and the Cup squads of 1952 and 1953, has won perhaps even greater honours as a coach. His most distinguished pupil is Rod Laver. Ian has coached Rod since Rod came down from Charlie Hollis in Rockhampton, a red-haired shaver of fourteen. Laver, though now working his way up the thorny professional path, still looks to Ayre for instruction. In the late 1950s and early 1960s Ayre coached the Queensland Linton Cup and Wilson Cup teams through an era of unprecedented success. He was Queensland Close champion in 1949, 1950 and 1952, toured South Africa with an Australian team in 1952 and was a member of the 1953 official Australian team to Europe and America. He played at Wimbledon in 1952 and 1953 and represented Australia in New Zealand in 1953. Ayre today commands a large radio following with his State, national title, and Davis Cup comments.

If you are in the late-thirty or over-forty age-group you can enjoy your tennis more than ever. The ex-champions do and so can you. They don't have to win any more. They can relax and play for fun again. They know the short cuts and now match their brains rather than their bodies. Remember the example of tennis's Rip Van Winkle, Pancho Segura, who was still beating the best at forty-two.

By the time you reach middle age, you have learnt to appreciate fully court positions and tactics. Before, tennis was a game in which you got out there and hit the ball. You had your tactics, sure. But you were young, impetuous and loved more than anything else to gallop madly around the court slamming winners. If you were caught out of position sometimes, so what! You had the energy to bounce back and crush your opponent.

Now the legs have slowed a little. You don't hurtle to the wings retrieving what your opponents fondly believed to be a winner. Your dash to the net has lost some of its zip, and those once capacious lungs can no longer store all the air you need. Now you start 'thinking' tennis and a new appreciation breeds a new love for the game.

The best tennis brain I ever struck belonged to Pancho Segura. He learnt from the acknowledged master, Bobby Riggs. And it was Segura's brain and knowledge which were largely responsible for the success of Pancho Gonzales.

You might be surprised that I have not nominated Harry Hopman as the Einstein of tennis. I think 'Hoppy's

Pancho Segura was still winning tournaments at the age of forty-two.

greatest assets are his tactical knowledge, and his ability to discipline, yet command, the respect of his players. When you were in Hopman's Davis Cup team you barely had to lift a finger. Distractions were not allowed to hinder your tennis. He was undoubtedly the greatest of all Davis Cup captains.

But you don't have to be a Segura, a Riggs or a Hopman to absorb tennis knowledge. Intelligent watching of tennis and post-mortems on your own game can teach you a lot.

I am still learning. Coaching has made me think tennis more than ever. Tennis is that sort of a game. In middle age, court-positioning and tactics become more important than ever, and it is wise to use a racket slightly lighter than when you were young. Obviously your reflexes will be slower and a lighter racket will help compensate for this. Don't go chasing every ball the way you once did. Your body will tell you that. It is the best guide to your physical capabilities. It will yell when it has had enough. But chase the important ones—for instance, when you have game or set point against you.

Even early in the match when you feel you have the energy, don't go scurrying for the minor points. You will need that dash for the last set. Remember to concentrate more on placements, vary the length and width of your shots, and use all the court in which to place them.

Make generous use of the lob, and thus try to keep your opponent retrieving. If he is in your age-bracket he may soon fold up. A shot to avoid is the half-volley. In your youth, you may have been a good volleyer. But don't let age lure you into the half-volley. One must have exceptionally powerful wrists to make this anything but a defensive shot.

I can't stress too much the importance of varying your strokes. During my world tour with the Australian team

Jack Crawford, as legend has that he always played, sleeves rolled down, long trousers and flat-topped racket in evidence.

in 1953, I had a few hits with the once great German player, Gottfried Von Cramm. He was a Wimbledon mixed-doubles champion in 1933. Twenty years later, he had me scrambling for his shots. Each one was different. Some carried top-spin some under-slice. Then he would chop or go for a hard flat drive. It reminded me of the time Harry Hopman nearly put the cleaners through me in Toowoomba. It was in the quarter-finals of the 1949 Australian hardcourt championships. I was nineteen, and you can guess how old 'Hoppy' was. He used all his wiles that day. One ball would stand up and look at me, the

next would fizz through like a rocket. I won in five sets but only because my legs were younger. Here was a perfect example of a tennis brain taking over from a tiring body.

A similar thing happened in the United States just after the war when Bobby Riggs, masterly American player and 1939 Wimbledon champion, met 'Big Bill' Tilden who ruled the Wimbledon courts in 1920–21 and again in 1930. They met in the final of a professional tournament, the best of three sets. Riggs won, but only after three exhausting sets of deciphering Tilden's chop, slice and spin. All the old champs resort to such tactics. Jack Crawford, the Wimbledon king of 1933, was another who could keep me guessing despite my twenty-two years age-advantage.

I knew a fellow in Brisbane—he started the game at fifty—who played once a week when he was eighty-three. He bought two new rackets a year and could hardly wait for his weekly outing on the court. Which brings us to those who take up tennis late—the housewives who can now be free of the family for a few hours a week, or the business man who has been ordered by the doctor into the open air. Remember the Golden Rules: (a) watch the ball. (b) Don't try to hit it too hard and (c) Maintain your balance.

Taking these rules in order: You must watch the ball or you will mis-hit it, or even miss it altogether. But watching the ball means watching it right on to your racket, not within a foot of it. I remember once in Sydney watching Rod Laver play Barry MacKay. Rod was on the way up and he was cutting MacKay to pieces. I was sitting with Vic Edwards, the Sydney coach, and after the first set, Vic said to me, 'the boy has it in the bag'. I said, 'I am not sure, Vic, I think he will lose.' I had noticed Rod start to look around between points. His concentration lapsed, and MacKay got up to win. The next time they met it was a five-setter, and with the pressure on him, Rod took the match.

In stroking the ball, remember to hit it on the rise. In this way you use your opponent's pace, save your own strength and get the ball back quicker. Hit as hard as you can, with control. A screaming return is no good at all unless controlled. Here is how you get control: Take a tight grip on the racket. Relax on the backswing and squeeze on your grip as you come in to make contact with the ball. Be careful not to tense up. Try and remember to gain a maximum squeeze without tensing. Try to make your back-swing while the ball is still in flight. Don't wait until it bounces or you will have to rush your shot.

Balance is something you can work out yourself. Don't worry so much about perfect positioning of the feet. We hound the kids about it, but they have plenty of time to sort themselves out. Remember to be comfortable—comfortable enough to be able to make your shot the way I have just explained.

To keep a good standard of tennis, I suggest you keep playing, if possible, on the same surface. If you are used to hardcourts, stick to them. The same if you are a grass-court player. The grass surface on which the ball fizzes off the court is faster than the hardcourt. Each surface demands special abilities to master it.

Harry Hopman bounds after a backhand return during the Melbourne Cricket Club's autumn tournament. Hopman played tournament tennis all around the world for more than 30 years. When his legs slowed, he compensated for it with shrewd tactics, guileful shotmaking.

24 THE GREATS OF AUSTRALIAN TENNIS
Jim Russell

Jim Russell is a short, oval-faced figure with a great thirst for travelling, mingling and yarning. Although he is best known as a comic-strip cartoonist, his activities in sport and entertainment have taken him to the far corners of the world. He has been an energetic tennis fan since 1936, was the Lawn Tennis Association of Australia's public relations adviser and president of the White City Tennis Club. He has made seven world tours, the first in 1939 when he accompanied the Australian team which won an astounding challenge round victory over America. He is Australian correspondent for the U.S.-owned World Tennis *magazine and with Sir Robert Menzies he is the only Australian to hold honorary life-membership of the U.S. International Lawn Tennis Club. He was chairman of publicity committees for the 1951, 1954 and 1960 challenge rounds in Sydney and captain-manager of the New South Wales tennis team in New Zealand in 1959. On and off for seventeen years, his cheery voice has gone out from radio and television stations in quiz shows and tennis broadcasts. Russell has been a life-long student of tennis and his home at Kangaroo Point, on Sydney's George's River, houses Australia's largest tennis library, part of it a gift from critic George McElhone.*

The identity of the man who brought tennis to Australia remains a mystery, but he seems likely to have been a scholar returning from Oxford or Cambridge. Not only would he have introduced Australians to the implements of the game, but to the rules of modern tennis set down by the Marylebone Cricket Club in London in 1875.

One early writer on the game, R.M. Kidston, suggested that the founder of the game in Australia was probably the father of Davis Cup player Pat O'Hara-Wood, but Pat told me not long before his death in 1961 that he doubted if this were true.

The first Wimbledon tournament had been played in 1877 and just three years later, in 1880, the first State championships were conducted in Victoria, with F. Highett winning the men's singles. New South Wales was five years behind Victoria, staging its first State titles in 1885 at the Sydney Cricket Ground, W.J. Salmon winning the men's singles. These State titles were followed by Queensland's first championships in 1889, South Australia's in 1890, Tasmania's in 1893 and Western Australia's in 1895. Thus, within fifteen years tennis swept to popularity in every Australian State.

Although these State Championships were the foundation of competitive tennis in Australia, it was the inter-state matches that began in New South Wales and Victoria in 1885—the same year the New South Wales titles began—that developed the spirit that ultimately pushed Australia into the front rank of the world's tennis nations.

The man who deserves greatest credit for the formation of a national tennis association was Thomas L. Hicks, first secretary of the Lawn Tennis Association of Aust-

Lew Hoad's entire body is poised on his toes as he tosses the ball up to serve. It was a service which worked well on all types of surfaces and was devastating at times.

ralia. Hicks was attracted to the Davis Cup competition, but the rules covering this great event said that challenges could come only from nations that had a national association. In 1904, Hicks decided to get one formed.

A year earlier, a young Victorian, Norman Everard Brookes, on a visit to England, had surprised many keen devotees of the game with his uncanny volleying skill. He had already made a reputation in Australia and had responded well to the teachings of an English player, Dr W. V. Eaves, who had played in Australia for the second time in 1902. A handsome New Zealander, Anthony Wilding, who was studying at Cambridge, had also shown in English tournaments that he was a world-class player.

With these two young men in mind, Hicks, who was secretary of the New South Wales L.T.A., convened a meeting of representatives from all States of Australia and from New Zealand. Only Western Australia did not attend the meeting in Sydney in September 1904, but Western Australia agreed to join if a national association was formed.

After these talks, another meeting was held in December 1904, and the Australasian Lawn Tennis Association, joining Australia and New Zealand as a tennis body, was formed. The way was clear for a challenge in the 1905 Davis Cup competition. W. H. Forrest became the first A.L.T.A. president.

For nearly sixty years, the fluctuations of Australian success in tennis have been reflected in our Davis Cup fortunes.

Anthony Wilding, informed in 1905 that he had been nominated to play in the Australasian team, said, 'Who my colleagues will be I do not know, but I hear that Brookes and Dunlop are coming and that Brookes is a dark horse.' They did not win that year and did not challenge in 1906.

Later, Hicks wrote to a friend telling him of his reaction to Australasia's winning the Davis Cup when it challenged

One of the fine teams which gave Australia world amateur tennis supremacy in the 1950s and early 1960s. *Left to right* Bob Mark, Neale Fraser, Harry Hopman, Rod Laver, and Roy Emerson. This side beat Italy 4–1 in the 1960 Challenge Round.

for only the second time in 1907. 'The winning of the Davis Cup in 1907 was not altogether a surprise to us after Brookes's successes on his first visit to England and the rapid strides made by Wilding,' he said.

But if it was no surprise to him and his colleagues, it was a deep shock to nations of the Northern Hemisphere. The rules for Davis Cup competition, providing that the Challenge Round should be played in the country of the holding nation, had boomeranged. They had been framed when only America and the British Isles were contestants, and now, whichever country won the right to challenge was faced with a six-months journey into regions of the world barely known to them.

In the fifty-seven years from 1905 when Australasia first challenged, to December 1962, when, as a single nation, Australia continued its modern domination of the Davis Cup competition by beating Mexico in the Brisbane Challenge Round, Australia or Australasia had won the Cup eighteen times, equalling the record of the U.S.A.

After winning the Cup at the second attempt in 1907, Australasia retained it in 1908 and 1909 and there was no challenge in 1910. In 1911, the matches were played at Christchurch, New Zealand, as a tribute to the part played in Australasia's victories by that city's native son Wilding. The Cup was retained then, but was lost in 1912 to Britain. The year 1913 saw the Australasians beaten in the first round by U.S.A. The Australasian team lacked both Wilding and Brookes, and America went on to win the Cup from Britain.

The following year, as war loomed, Australasia recovered the Cup, but did not take it home. Because German raiders were causing havoc among allied shipping it was felt that the trophy would be safer in the vaults of Black, Starr and Frost, in New York, and there it stayed until after the war.

Davis Cup contests were resumed in 1919 and Australasia retained the Cup in Sydney by beating Britain. But, with the re-entry of the U.S. in 1920 and the introduction of William Tilden and William Johnson to the competition, the Cup returned to the home of its donor. Australia was destined not to see it again for twenty years.

In 1922, Australia and New Zealand decided to go it alone in Cup contest, so that in 1923 Australia challenged for the first time as a single nation. But because of lack of cash and lack of outstanding players, Australia did not challenge in 1926, 1927, 1929, and 1931.

However, new faces had appeared in Australian tennis. Among these was the big, hard-hitting Victorian, Gerald Patterson, a nephew of Dame Nellie Melba, who crashed through the first Wimbledon after World War I to win the singles title at his first attempt. Patterson was brilliant when hitting winners, but his game often was a mixture of

124

great shots and wild errors. The story is told of a man who had never watched tennis before being shown the ferocious looking Australian at Wimbledon. After the match, he was asked, 'Well, what do you think of him?' The amazed newcomer replied, 'He hits very hard, but I should imagine he usually plays on a much bigger court!' Patterson's strength lay in the great power of his forehand drives, volleys and smashes which were virtually untakeable. With this armoury, he won the Wimbledon title in 1919 and 1922 and became heir apparent to Brookes soon to retire.

James O. Anderson, from Sydney, also had limited stroke equipment, and played from the base-line. From 1919 to 1925, the team of Patterson and Anderson led Australia's fruitless attack on the American-held Davis Cup defended by Tilden and Johnston. Patterson represented Australia again in 1928, but Anderson's last Davis Cup match was in 1925. Two other fine players of that era were Par O'Hara-Wood, who starred in doubles in 1920, 1922 and 1924, and J. B. Hawkes, who represented Australia in 1921, 1923 and 1925.

By 1939, Australia had built up a splendid team—John Bromwich and Adrian Quist—and, on the departure to professional tennis of Donald Budge, Australia at last won the Davis Cup again. But, again a world war deprived Australia full benefits of victory, and seven years passed before the competition was resumed. Then a virile six-man U.S. team, headed by Jack Kramer and Ted Schroeder smashed Australia's hopes of holding the Cup until new, young players had been built up. This took until 1950 when Frank Sedgman and Ken McGregor helped by the deep experience of John Bromwich and the shrewdness of non-playing captain Harry Hopman, won the Cup from America at Forest Hills in three straight rubbers.

Thus, the stage was set in Australia for what has become the most prolonged domination of world tennis by one country in the history of tennis. France had held the Davis Cup for six years straight from 1927 until they lost to Britain in 1933. Before this, America had been dominant in Cup competition from 1921 until their loss to France in 1927.

Australia, in its long run of successes after World War II, twice lost the Davis Cup to the U.S., the first time in 1954 and the second in 1958, but the Cup was regained convincingly within eight months each time—and Australian domination resumed as though continuity of

Ellsworth Vines and Jack Crawford, right, enter the Wimbledon centre court for their 1933 final, often ranked the finest this great tournament has produced. Crawford's returning of Vines' cannonball service enabled him to hold the American until gradually his guileful game assumed control.

Don Budge, first man to complete the grand slam of the world's four major tournaments, began his 'slam' by winning the Australian singles. Laver emulated him 24 years later.

success had been unbroken. From 1950 to 1962, thirteen Davis Cup competitions were played, and Australia won eleven.

Meanwhile, in world tournaments Frank Sedgman, Lewis Hoad, Ashley Cooper, Neale Fraser and Rod Laver won the Wimbledon singles (Hoad and Laver each twice). There were all-Australian finals at Wimbledon six times in the nine years to 1963 when 'Chuck' McKinley beat Australia's Fred Stolle.

Frank Sedgman also became the first Australian to win the U.S. singles when he beat Vic Seixas in the 1951 final. He repeated the victory the following year by beating Gardnar Mulloy. In winning these finals, Sedgman lost only twelve games, six in each match.

From 1956 to 1962, the U.S. title, which for so long had eluded the greatest Australians, has seen an all-Australian final each year excepting 1959, with no less than five Australians winning the event. These are Rosewall, Cooper, Anderson, Fraser (twice) and Laver (twice).

In 1962, Laver capped this complete domination of amateur tennis by winning the grand slam—the singles championships of Australia, Wimbledon, France and the U.S. in one year, The feat had only once before been achieved—by American Donald Budge in 1938, but Laver went one better than Budge by winning the Italian title, too!

The honour-boards of Australian tennis bear the names of many colourful personalities. The first outstanding Australian champion was Dudley Webb, of Victoria who, dominated the game in the middle 1880s. According to historians, he was almost unbeatable until a new star, Ben Green, also a Victorian, emerged. Webb, who by this time was living in New South Wales, was noted for his ground-strokes, while Green was a brilliant volleyer. Hence the 'Victorian' game was the volleying style, while the 'New South Wales' game featured the base-liner. Webb and Green had many great matches with crowds of 2,000 or 3,000 attending the New South Wales championships in May each year. R. M. Kidston, who wrote under the pen-name of 'Austral' in the *Sydney Referee,* recorded: 'On one occasion, Green and Webb were struck with cramps almost at the same instant, to their own great discomfort, but to the laughter of the crowd, although they sympathised.'

The first Australian championship in 1905 was won by Rodney Heath. Others who stood out were Leslie Gaden, of New South Wales, and Alf Dunlop, of Victoria, both fine doubles players. They were joined later by impish Horrie Rice, of Sydney, who played in knee-length knickerbockers, with black socks—quite as revolutionary in those days as shorts became later. Rice played for Australia in the 1913 Davis Cup.

The emergence of Norman Brookes as a great player marked the coming-of-age of Australia as a tennis nation and, by joining forces with Wilding, he started the boom which is still evident. Brookes, who was knighted in 1939, played in nine Davis Cup competitions from 1905 to 1920. He was a cold, analytical player whose grim visage never relaxed into a smile to make his opponent more comfortable. He was the first left-hander to upset the opposing

champions by taking the rising ball and moving swiftly to the net, from where he sent down uncanny volleys.

In the next few years, L. O. S. Poidevin, R. W. Heath, S. N. Doust (who later lived in England where he became a famous tennis writer), A. B. Jones and N. Peach won places in Australian teams.

On to the Australian tennis stage in the decade after World War I came Clarrie Todd, 'Sos' Wertheim, Bob Schlesinger, Ian McInness, Fred Kalms, 'Gar' Moon and Jim Willard, all of whom represented their country in Davis Cup matches. R. O. Cummings, also, was a familiar figure who played tennis for Australia in the Olympic Games. But it was not until the rise of the young Sydney player, Jack Crawford, late in the 1920s, that Australia developed a competitor to bring back glories of the past. With his fluent stylish stroking, powerful forehand and smooth, sliced backhand, Crawford soon rose to the top.

Realizing that if the younger players like Harry Hopman were to gain the experience needed to compete against the world's best, the L.T.A.A. headed by its president, Norman Brookes, invited the great French players, Jean Borotra, Jacques Brugnon and Christian Boussus, to Australia. In 1932, the L.T.A.A. also brought out the reigning Wimbledon title-holder, Ellsworth Vines, with his fellow-Americans, Keith Gledhill, John Van Ryn and Wilmer Allison. Against them Crawford was impressive. He emerged from these matches as a potential world champion, a position he reached in 1933, when he took the Wimbledon singles from the defending champion, Vines. This match is still spoken of as possibly the greatest-ever Wimbledon final.

In 1933, Crawford had already won the Australian and French titles, and had only to take the U.S. singles to become the first man in history to win the four major titles of the world in one year. But he was stale—mentally exhausted—by the time he met Englishman Fred Perry in the final, and although leading by two sets to one at the interval, he slumped badly and lost the last two sets.

Closely behind Crawford were two youngsters, Vivian McGrath, of Sydney, and Adrian Quist, of Adelaide. McGrath introduced the double-handed shot into top tennis. Quist was more orthodox, and although short in stature, not only took the Australian singles title in 1936, 1940 and 1948, but became one of the world's all-time great doubles players. He won the Wimbledon doubles title twice—in 1935 with Crawford, and fifteen years later with Bromwich.

McGrath was probably one of the three greatest juniors the game has ever known. The others, I believe, were America's Vincent Richards and Frank Parker. McGrath's magnificent play against Vines and Allison at the age of sixteen in 1932, when he beat both players, and against Fred Perry a year later, stamped him as a phenomenon. But continuous overseas tours at too early an age appeared to burn up his enthusiasm, and after the outbreak of war in 1939, he dropped out of the game completely.

Others who played for Australia during the 1930s were Jack Clemenger, Don Turnbull, Len Schwartz and Cliff

Sproule, who, after the war, became a tennis administrator. Sproule has been referee of every Challenge Round held in Australia since 1951—surely a record unequalled elsewhere.

In 1935, another two-hander, John Bromwich, appeared. He was chosen for his first Davis Cup tour in 1937, and until 1950 missed only one Cup team—in 1948 —when he chose not to go.

In 1939, Quist and Bromwich, playing singles and doubles, won the Cup from U.S.A. at Merion, Philadelphia, in the most dramatic circumstances. As in 1914, war was declared while the competition was in progress. This time, however, the declaration of war by England against Germany was made while the actual Challenge Round was being played. Equally as dramatic were the circumstances in which Australia won the tie. Although strongly favoured to win, Quist and Bromwich were beaten by Frank Parker and Bobby Riggs on the opening day. Thus, to take the Cup Australia had to win the remaining three rubbers in the next two days, a feat never before or since achieved in a Challenge Round. Quist and Bromwich beat Jack Kramer and Joe Hunt in the doubles. Then Quist turned on superlative tennis to beat Riggs, while Bromwich mercilessly beat Parker in three straight sets.

The Quist and Bromwich who played the doubles in the Challenge Round in Melbourne in 1946, when Cup contests were resumed, were shadows of the pre-war pair, but they continued to play together and, in 1950, playing as a pair at Wimbledon for the first time, won the title. I believe, from studying their records, and from discussions I have had with many players of the past and present, that Quist and Bromwich rank as the greatest doubles pair in the history of tennis.

Immediately after the World War II, Australia took second place to the U.S.A., but reached the Challenge Round each year. In these early post-war years, Dinny Pails, Colin Long, Geoff. Brown (another two-hander) and Bill Sidwell each played in at least two Cup competitions, but Kramer and Schroeder, aided later by Pancho Gonzales, with Bill Talbert and Gardnar Mulloy in doubles, were too strong.

However, new champions were rising in Australian junior tennis—Frank Sedgman, George Worthington, Mervyn Rose and Ken McGregor—and in 1950 the L.T.A.A. sent this young team, with John Bromwich, and with Harry Hopman as non-playing captain, to try to do what the others had failed to do.

There was a sensation when Hopman named his singles players for the Challenge Round. Instead of Bromwich as second singles to Sedgman, as was expected, Hopman nominated the tall hard-hitting McGregor. Sedgman beat Tom Brown in the opener and most spectators believed that Schroeder would equalize by beating the young newcomer. But McGregor defeated the American in straight sets, after a first set of twenty-four games. Next day, Bromwich and Sedgman defeated Schroeder and Mulloy in five sets—and the Cup was back in Australia. This began the golden era that reached its climax in 1954 when a world record crowd of 25,578 spectators

The late Sir Norman Brookes, former Wimbledon Champion, Davis Cup Star, and first President of The Lawn Tennis Association of Australia.

attended daily for three days at the White City Courts in Sydney and watched the American two-man team, Tony Trabert and Vic Seixas, take the trophy back to its homeland—temporarily.

Sedgman, Rose and McGregor, led again by Harry Hopman, had successfully turned back a determined challenge from the U.S. in 1951 in Sydney, and a year later in Adelaide, Sedgman and McGregor, playing singles and doubles, had repeated the performance. A few days later, both players, not unexpectedly, announced that they had turned professional, and had joined the promotional activities of Jack Kramer. This threw the burden of defending the Cup in that record 1953 tie on the two nineteen-year-olds, Rosewall and Hoad. Early in the year, Rosewall, at eighteen, had shown his potential by winning the Australian singles, the youngest player

Daphne Ackurst, one of the pioneer players who persisted with the development of their sport at a time when they might easily have given it up because of lack of support from officials.

ever to achieve that honour. A few months later in Paris, while still eighteen, he carried off the French singles with tennis of such brilliance that it drew praise from the 'Four Musketeers' of French tennis—Lacoste, Cochet, Borotra and Brugnon—who watched the final against Seixas. Rosewall was the youngest player ever to win that title too.

But after Rosewall's defeat at Wimbledon by Kurt Nielson—partly caused by illness, partly by weariness from play and travel and over-exposure to the strain of No 1 seeding—doubts began to grow about whether he and Hoad would be stale by the time the Challenge Round opened in December 1953 at Kooyong courts in Melbourne. The story of how the two youngsters fought back from being two-one down after the first three rubbers to win both singles and the Cup in their debut in this competition is legend now. Overnight, they became heroes.

Australia lost the trophy in 1954, but eight months later, Hoad, Rosewall and Rex Hartwig recovered it with a 5–0 win over the U.S.A. in America.

In 1956, Hoad and Rosewall went through to the Wimbledon final after Hoad had already won the Australian and French titles. When he beat Rosewall in the Wimbledon match, he was all set to be the first Australian to win the grand slam. But a tenacious Rosewall stopped this by beating him for the U.S. title, and set the stage for a triumphant exit from amateur ranks.

In the years that followed, Ashley Cooper, Mal Anderson and Neale Fraser represented Australia with great distinction and won major titles everywhere.

One of the saddest spectacles for Australian tennis fans was the 1958 Challenge Round in Brisbane, when Anderson and Cooper had both made agreements with Jack Kramer to turn professional immediately after the matches. But so disconcerted were they by the problems on their minds, and the harassing they were receiving, that the Americans won the Cup. However, with Neale Fraser spearheading the attack, and Rod Laver as second singles string, and Roy Emerson aiding brilliantly in doubles, Australia regained the Cup after only a few months.

From this time on, Kramer's raids on Australian tennis deprived rising competitors of the chance of regular games against the best players in the world, but Australia's virile tennis organization has continued to produce new crops of outstanding players.

In 1960 and 1961, Italy gained the right to challenge, but was decisively turned back. In 1962, the Mexicans put up a more spirited challenge, even though they lost 5–0. This time, Laver turned professional after the Challenge Round, and Fraser retired from active competition. Only time will tell if their loss can be overcome by determined youngsters and good administration.

No story of Australian tennis would be complete without saying something of the great role played by Harry Hopman. Ask any five people for their assessment of Hopman, and you will get five different answers, so it is difficult to quote any generally accepted view of him. And Hopman, himself, isn't much help in making an assessment, either, because he isn't greatly interested in whether you like him, dislike him or ignore him. How-

ever, the facts, at least, can be put down.

He was born on 12 August 1906 in Sydney, and by the time he was nearing nineteen, he had established himself as an outstanding junior. He was selected to tour in the Davis Cup teams of 1928, 1930 and 1932, when teams were sent only every second year. By 1933, he had begun to drop back in rankings to make room for players like McGrath, Quist and Turnbull, but when a player with managerial capabilities was to be chosen for the 1938 team (Bromwich, Quist and Schwartz were the others), Hopman got the job. His dedication to physical fitness, and the shrewdness he brought to the captaincy, helped in gaining Australia a place in the challenge round and ensured him the same post the next year, 1939, when his team won the Cup.

After the war, others were preferred to him as captains and managers, but he had been working quietly on the development of the modern game of serve and volley, and had been helping in the training programme of young players like Sedgman and McGregor. He was selected as non-playing captain in 1950. Some say that he quietly waited until he believed he had a potential winning team, and had chosen that year. If this is true, it simply highlights the ability that Hopman has to pick winners, for that was the year the Cup was regained. Since that time, Hopman was undisputed first choice to captain Australia's Davis Cup teams, and he built up a record of captaining twelve winning teams against only three losses in the fifteen ties. With the three other teams in which he played (but not as captain), Hopman represented Australia in eighteen competitions—a record that may never be broken. Harry Hopman resigned as captain of the Australian Davis Cup team in February 1969 and now lives in the U.S.A. where he is head coach of the Port Washington Tennis Academy, Long Island, New York.

Hopman has been called a martinet, a Simon Legree, and many other harsh things by players and newspapermen. Players have often writhed under his discipline, yet later the same men have spoken highly of his thoughtfulness and consideration. Some newspaper-men will tell you many things that they know in his disfavour; yet I have often seen him help young journalists.

Whatever you think of Hopman, he is the type of controversial figure who cannot be ignored. I doubt whether an accurate portrait of him will ever be possible. Today, thirty-eight years after first meeting him, I feel less able than ever to summarize him. But this I will say: In the history of Australian tennis, many people have played their parts, but two figures stand out head and shoulders above the others for the impact they have made on the game. One is Sir Norman Brookes who was born in 1877, the year that the first lawn-tennis championships were played at Wimbledon; the other is Hopman, who was born the year that Brookes was playing in his sixth Davis Cup.

Both have been Australian champions in other sports. Sir Norman twice won the golf foursomes of Australia; Hopman was four times squash champion of Australia. Each, in his way, has played a tremendous part as an architect of the Australian tennis structure. And, after Hopman, who will be the next strong figure?